T0170820

Cowboys
Triviology

Christopher Walsh

TRIUMPH
BOOKS

For the man who seemingly does everything big, Jonathan Harder.

"There are no traffic jams along the extra mile."

—Roger Staubach

Library of Congress Cataloging-in-Publication Data

Walsh, Christopher J., 1968–
  Cowboys triviology / by Christopher Walsh.
      p. cm.
  ISBN 978-1-60078-622-8
  1. Dallas Cowboys (Football team)—Juvenile literature. I. Title.
  GV956.D3W35 2011
  796.332'64097642812—dc22
                                2011007216

This book is available in quantity at special discounts for your group or organization. For further information, contact:

   Triumph Books LLC
   814 North Franklin Street
   Chicago, Illinois 60610
   www.triumphbooks.com

Printed in U.S.A.
ISBN: 978-1-60078-622-8
Design by Patricia Frey
Photos courtesy of AP Images except where otherwise noted.

Contents

Introduction

It gives me great pleasure to be able to finally do this.

During the 1998 and 1999 NFL seasons, I was covering the Arizona Cardinals for the *Tucson Citizen*, along with three other daily news outlets (which will tell you something about how things have changed during the past dozen years). One of those was the *Arizona Republic*, which had Steve Schoenfeld as a reporter.

Steve was nothing short of amazing. Relentless as a reporter, he worked sources better than anyone I knew and was simultaneously encouraging to those of us who weren't as experienced. Among his numerous passions—including waking up colleagues early in the morning with, "Hi. This is Steve," and then following with something like, "Did you see this?"—was food, especially discovering good restaurants on the road. For example, while he hated visiting Philadelphia, he absolutely adored its restaurants.

Steve was a legend who had also worked for newspapers in Dallas, Tulsa, and his native Kansas, as well as serving as the president of the Pro Football Writers Association from 1997 to 1999.

On October 24, 2000, after I'd moved on to cover the Green Bay Packers and Steve had accepted a job with CBSSportsline.com, he was crossing a street in Tempe after attending a speech by Helen

Thomas, the former UPI White House correspondent, and was killed by a hit-and-run driver.

He was 45. The following weekend, when the NFL honored him with a moment of silence in all press boxes before each of its games, I was in Miami still trying to numb my sorrow. I think Steve would have been proud of me—or at least I thought of him—when I was the only reporter to find out that during the key play of the game the wrong player was on the field for the Packers.

I don't bring this up because he once worked for the *Dallas Times-Herald*, or was a friend and colleague who is sorely missed, but for the following, simple reason:

Jerry Jones, owner of the Dallas Cowboys, provided his airplane for reporters to attend the funeral, which was held in the middle of the NFL season, when it's pretty much impossible to get away even for a day. I wasn't among the group, but have always hoped to find some way to publicly thank him for that very generous gesture.

Now on to the book.

In putting this together my aim wasn't to be overly difficult or have it serve as a quiz to measure the football IQ of even the most die-hard fans, but rather to celebrate, honor, and inform. The Dallas Cowboys are one of the most remarkable pro franchises to have ever existed, and sometimes it's hard to believe that the team has been playing for just 50-odd years.

Although it's seemingly developed into a Super Bowl–or–bust organization, few can argue that from the cheerleaders to the ownership the one thing that it does better than just about anything else is attract attention.

Seriously, have you seen or been in Cowboys Stadium? Yikes. You could show a movie on the video screen and watch it in Mississippi.

The book is organized into sections to make it easy to use. At times it breaks down into subsections, such as Super Bowls or Hall of Fame players. The questions range in difficulty from very easy to extremely difficult, and those in the Two-Minute Drill are borderline impossible. Answers are given at the end of each section.

Above all else, I hope you enjoy the book and learn a few things along the way.

Dallas Cowboys head coach Tom Landry watches the action. *(Getty Images)*

One

The Basics

In 1958, three wealthy Texas oilmen were looking to purchase struggling teams in the National Football League and move them to the Lone Star State, only to fail at landing the Cardinals and Redskins franchises, in addition to being rebuffed in their efforts to form new teams.

The men were Bud Adams, Lamar Hunt, and Clint Murchison.

When George Halas of the Chicago Bears, who had tremendous influence at the time, insisted that the NFL would remain a 12-team league, Hunt decided to challenge it and spearheaded the American Football League. While the NFL didn't have a presence in Texas, the AFL planned to immediately have two teams, Hunt's Dallas Texans and Adams' Houston Oilers. This in addition to franchises in Boston, Buffalo, Denver, Los Angeles, and New York.

Needless to say, the NFL took immediate notice, especially after the AFL signed a five-year television contract with ABC, for which each team received $150,000. Six months later, during the owners' meetings in Palm Beach, the NFL countered by awarding an expansion franchise in Hunt's backyard and subsequently added the Minnesota Vikings, which was originally going to join the AFL as its Midwestern anchor (but instead opened the door for Oakland), a year later.

Consequently, the Dallas Cowboys joined the NFL on January 28, 1960, with Murchison the majority owner in partnership with attorney Bedford Wynne. Murchison was 37 years old, and Wynne 46. One of their first moves was to hire Tex Schramm as team president and general manager, and he brought in Gil Brandt as the team's original scouting director.

The idea was that it would take years for the upstart team to be competitive, supported by a solid financial base. Between that and the brief time period to prepare for the 1960 season, the Cowboys were the only NFL expansion team not to have had the benefit of a draft its first year, but owners shrewdly made a couple of key signings to binding personal-services contracts before the team was officially created.

1. What's the logo of the Dallas Cowboys?
2. What does it represent?
3. True or false? The logo always had the outlining trim.
4. Before settling on the nickname Cowboys, what two other nicknames were considered?
5. What was the headline in the *Dallas Morning News* on December 29, 1959?
6. What was Tom Landry known for wearing along the sideline?
7. True or false? Tom Landry's 29 years with the same NFL team set an NFL coaching record.
8. How many Cowboys have their numbers retired? List them.
9. What year did the Cowboys begin the tradition of playing on Thanksgiving Day?
10. True or false? Dallas shut out its opponent when it debuted on *Monday Night Football.*
11. True or false? The Cowboys actually played five times on a Monday before *Monday Night Football* existed.
12. Who was known as Mr. Cowboy?
13. Name the two Cowboys named the Walter Payton Man of the Year.
14. Who is the only Dallas player to be named league MVP and also won the Super Bowl during the same season?
15. Who was the only Dallas Cowboy to be named the NFL Defensive Player of the Year by the Associated Press? (Bonus: Name the year.)
16. True or false? Dallas was in half of the Super Bowls played in the 1970s.
17. Which occurred first, Bob Lilly being enshrined in the Pro Football Hall of Fame or Roger Staubach announcing his retirement?
18. When Dallas set the NFL record with its 17th-straight winning season in 1982, which team previously had the record?

19. In 1983, where did the Cowboys break ground on a new headquarters and training facility?
20. Outside of Tom Landry, which head coach was with the Cowboys the longest?
21. What was Bill Parcells' nickname?
22. True or false? Dallas celebrated its 25ᵗʰ anniversary in 1984 by winning the Super Bowl.
23. True or false? The Cowboys have held training camp at home in Dallas.
24. In what year, and where, did the Cowboys hold their first in-state training camp?
25. True or false? Owner Jerry Jones tried to purchase the San Diego Chargers in 1967.
26. What connection did Jerry Jones and Jimmy Johnson have prior to the Cowboys?
27. What color jerseys does Dallas prefer to wear and why?
28. True or false? Since then the team motto has been "Good guys wear white."
29. Who were the triplets?
30. True or false? The Cowboys have always had cheerleaders like they do now at home games.
31. True or false? The Cowboys sold out every game, home and away, during the 1990s.
32. Who coined the term "America's Team" for the Cowboys?
33. True or false? Tom Landry initially didn't like the America's Team moniker because he thought it would inspire opponents.
34. What was the most number of wins in a season the Cowboys enjoyed during their first five seasons?
35. If the Cowboys are American's Team, what are the Dallas Cowboys cheerleaders?

Answers:

1. A blue star.
2. Texas is considered the Lone Star State.
3. False. Originally it was the blue star by itself.
4. Steers and Rangers.
5. "Rangers Hire Tom Landry"
6. A fedora.
7. True
8. Dallas has never retired a number.
9. 1966. Dallas defeated Cleveland, 26–14.
10. False. It lost to St. Louis 38–0 on November 16, 1970.
11. True. Its first Monday game was in 1965, when Dallas lost to St. Louis, 20–13. The Cowboys were 2–3 on Mondays before *Monday Night Football* was created in 1970.
12. Defensive lineman Bob Lilly.
13. Roger Staubach in 1978 and Troy Aikman in 1997.
14. Emmitt Smith in 1993.
15. Harvey Martin in 1977.
16. True. The Cowboys went 2–3.
17. Roger Staubach announced his retirement on March 31, 1980, while Bob Lilly was enshrined on August 2 of that same year.
18. The Oakland Raiders were the first team in NFL history to have 16-straight winning seasons.
19. Valley Ranch in northwest Dallas County. It opened a year later.
20. Jimmy Johnson, five years (1989–93).
21. The Big Tuna.
22. False. The Cowboys finished 9–7 and missed the playoffs for the first time in 10 years.
23. False
24. 1990 at St. Edward's University in Austin.
25. True
26. They were roommates at the University of Arkansas.
27. White. Tex Schramm decided to have the team wear white at home in order to present fans with a consistent look.
28. False
29. Troy Aikman, Emmitt Smith, and Michael Irvin.
30. False. The Cowboys have always had cheerleaders, but not always like the ones currently on the sidelines. The famous unit that resembles a dance line was introduced at Texas Stadium in 1972.
31. False, but the Cowboys were close. Dallas had a streak of 160 sold-out home and away games, including playoffs, which began on December 23, 1990, at Philadelphia's Veterans Stadium and was snapped December 24, 1999 against New Orleans in the Louisiana Superdome.
32. Bob Ryan, the future vice president and editor-in-chief of NFL Films, coined the term "America's Team" while preparing and editing the Cowboys' 1978 season-highlight film.
33. True
34. Five. Despite that, Tom Landry was still given a contract extension.
35. America's Sweethearts.

Two

League History

It all goes back to 1869 and the campuses of two rival Ivy League schools, when Rutgers and Princeton decided to play each other in a new sport that was a hybrid of soccer and rugby, but looked more like an organized riot. On November 6, they met using modified London Football Association rules and Rutgers won 6–4 despite one of its professors pointing his umbrella at participants and yelling, "You will come to no Christian end." There were roughly 100 people in attendance.

From there the game quickly began to evolve, with Walter Camp, considered the father of American football, setting down rules in 1876 and continuing to revise them until his death in 1925. His numerous innovations included one side potentially having undisputed possession of the ball until it gave it up or scored, and reducing the number of players on the field from 15 to 11. He also created the quarterback and center positions in addition to the forward pass.

Camp, who played and coached at Yale, also standardized scoring. In 1892, the equivalent of a field goal was five points, one more than a touchdown. A goal following a touchdown was two points, as was a safety. It wasn't until 1912, eight years before the creation of the National Football League, that a touchdown was rewarded with six points and a field goal three.

While football became a major attraction for local athletic clubs, with the Allegheny Athletic Association and Pittsburgh Athletic Club credited with having the first professionals, the first attempt at a pro league was made in 1902 when baseball's Philadelphia Athletics (managed by Connie Mack) and Philadelphia Phillies formed pro football teams, joining the Pittsburgh Stars.

After years of unsettled confusion—with salaries rising, players jumping from team to team and college athletes being used while still in school—an organizational meeting was held in 1920 at the Jordan and Humpmobile auto showroom in Canton, Ohio, to begin drawing up plans for a centralized league with one set of rules, the American Professional Football Conference. Two years later, the APFA changed its name to the National Football League.

The rest, as they say, is history.

Cowboys defensive end George Andrie scoops up a Bart Starr fumble in the Ice Bowl, December 31, 1967.

1. A major reason for the creation of the Dallas Cowboys was for it to directly compete with which AFL franchise?
2. At the same meeting in Palm Beach during which the Cowboys were granted an expansion franchise, who was voted league commissioner?
3. How many Dallas Cowboys were in the initial Pro Football Hall of Fame class elected in 1963?
4. True or false? Just after winning the AFL championship, the Dallas Texans moved to Kansas City and were renamed the Chiefs.
5. True or false? The precursor to the AFL-NFL merger were a series of secret springtime meetings between Kansas City Chiefs owner Lamar Hunt and Tex Schramm, with NFL commissioner Pete Rozelle announcing the completed deal on June 8, 1966.
6. What was the temperature of the 1967 NFL Championship Game, nicknamed the Ice Bowl, in Green Bay?
7. When did the Dallas Cowboys make their first appearance in the Hall of Fame game and against what opponent?
8. True or false? Walter Payton set a single-game rushing record with 275 yards against Dallas in 1977.
9. How many consecutive Super Bowls had the NFC lost before Dallas defeated Denver in Super Bowl XII?
10. During ESPN's first year broadcasting NFL games, 1987, which team did Dallas host when the game drew a 10.2 cable rating in 4.36 million homes?
11. What was Tex Schramm named the president of in 1989?
12. Who succeeded him?
13. Who was the first head coach in NFL history to guide four different teams to the playoffs?

14. True or false? When the Cleveland Browns played for the first time since 1995 they defeated the Cowboys 20–17 in overtime at the 1999 Hall of Fame Game.

15. True or false? Heading into the 2010 season, Dallas had more Monday wins than any other team in the NFL.

16. True or false? The Cowboys had the league's best winning percentage on *Monday Night Football*.

17. How many times has a Dallas Cowboy been named the Associated Press' Defensive Rookie of the Year?

18. How much did H.R. "Bum" Bright buy the Dallas Cowboys for in 1984?

19. How much did he sell it for five years later?

20. True or false? H.R. "Bum" Bright had to sell the team to settle his divorce.

21. How did they settle the final $300,000 of the deal?

22. True or false? H.R. "Bum" Bright later purchased a two-headed quarter from a magic shop and sent it to Jerry Jones with the note "You'll never know," as a joke.

23. Which league innovation was applied to every team at the end of the 1993 season?

24. Who is the only player in NFL history to gain 4,000 yards three different ways (rushing, receiving, and kickoff returning)?

25. Which Cowboys were named to the NFL's All-Decade Team in the 1960s?

26. Which Cowboys were named to the NFL's All-Decade Team in the 1970s?

27. Which Cowboys were named to the NFL's All-Decade Team in the 1980s?

28. Which Cowboys were named to the NFL's All-Decade Team in the 1990s?

29. Which Cowboys were named to the NFL's All-Decade Team in the 2000s?

Answers:

1. The Dallas Texans.
2. Pete Rozelle
3. None. The Cowboys were three years old.
4. True. The Dallas Texans defeated the Houston Oilers 20–17 after 17 minutes and 54 seconds of overtime on a 25-yard field goal by Tommy Brooker.
5. True
6. 13 below zero.
7. 1968, Dallas lost to the Chicago Bears, 30–24.
8. False. He did it against Minnesota.
9. Five
10. The Los Angeles Raiders.
11. The World League of American Football, with a six-man committee comprised of Dan Rooney, Norman Braman, Lamar Hunt, Victor Kiam, Mike Lynn, and Bill Walsh.
12. Mike Lynn, general manager of the Minnesota Vikings.
13. Bill Parcells, the fourth being the Cowboys in 2003.
14. True
15. True. The Cowboys were 42–29.
16. False. Pittsburgh, Indianapolis, Seattle and San Francisco all had winning percentages above .600.
17. Zero
18. $80 million.
19. $140 million.
20. False, it was primarily due to the failure of his bank, Republic Bank.
21. Coin flip. Jerry Jones lost.
22. True
23. The salary cap.
24. Herschel Walker.
25. Tackle Ralph Neely and defensive tackle Bob Lilly. Cornerback Herb Adderley was also selected, but spent more time with the Green Bay Packers.
26. Wide receiver Drew Pearson, quarterback Roger Staubach, tackle Rayfield Wright, defensive tackle Bob Lilly and safety Cliff Harris were all first-team selections. Defensive end Harvey Martin was a second-team pick.
27. Defensive tackle Randy White was the only selection.
28. Running back Emmitt Smith and cornerback/punt returner Deion Sanders were first-team selections. Second-team picks were wide receiver Michael Irvin, guard Larry Allen, and tackle Mark Stepnoski.
29. The Cowboys didn't have any first-team selections. Second-team picks (those who at least played briefly with Dallas) were wide receiver Terrell Owens, guard Larry Allen, defensive tackle La'Roi Glover, linebacker Zach Thomas, and linebacker DeMarcus Ware.

Three

Famous Firsts

In the late 1950s, the National Football League's popularity was beginning to soar and rival baseball as the nation's top sport. Attendance went from 1.98 million in 1950 to more than 3 million in 1958 despite having just a dozen teams.

The league actually began the decade with 13 teams, only to have the Baltimore Colts fold and the New York Yanks become the Dallas Texans in 1952. But when that franchise failed to catch on it moved to Baltimore, and this time the Colts took hold.

Few grasped that Texas, Dallas specifically, was about to become the front line of professional football, with teams from both the NFL and upstart American Football League fighting to control one of the nation's biggest and fastest-growing markets.

Not only were the Dallas Cowboys the NFL's first southern franchise, but the first modern-era expansion team. Within 10 years, the league would go from those 12 franchises to 26.

1. True or false? When Tom Landry was hired he was immediately named the first head coach of the Dallas Cowboys.
2. Where did Dallas hold its first training camp?
3. True or false? The Cowboys won their first preseason game. (Bonus: Name where it was played)
4. True or false? The Cowboys won their first home preseason game.
5. Against what future Super Bowl opponent was the first regular season game played?
6. What was the first non-loss in franchise history?
7. What was the Cowboys' record in their inaugural season?
8. Which NFL statistical category did Dallas lead in its first season?
9. Who did the Cowboys record their first victory against?
10. True or false? In 1962, Dallas became the first team in league history to record two 100-yard touchdowns not only in the same season, but in the same quarter.
11. What was unique about the contract extension Tom Landry signed in 1964, with one year left on his deal?
12. In what year did the Cowboys enjoy their first home sellout?
13. When did Dallas capture its first championship? (Note: championship does not necessarily mean Super Bowl).
14. Who was the MVP of Super Bowl V, Dallas' first Super Bowl appearance?
15. Who did the Cowboys select when they had the first selection in the NFL Draft for the first time in 1974? (Bonus: Who did they trade to get the pick and to which team?)
16. Who was the first player inducted into the Ring of Honor at Texas Stadium?
17. Who was the first Dallas Cowboys player to score two touchdowns on returns of any kind in the same game?
18. Who was the last original Dallas Cowboy to retire?

Answers:

1. False, although it's a bit of a trick question. When Clint Murchison, Jr., and Bedford Wynne signed New York Giants defensive assistant Tom Landry, it was to a personal services contract on December 27, 1959, with the intention of naming him head coach once they were officially awarded an expansion franchise.
2. The first training camp was held at Pacific University in Forest Grove, Oregon. It opened on July 9, 1960.
3. False. The Cowboys lost their first preseason game 16–10 to the San Francisco 49ers in Seattle.
4. False. Heading into the final minute Dallas led the world champion Baltimore Colts before Johnny Unitas connected with Lenny Moore for a 62-yard completion for a 14–10 victory on August 19, 1960.
5. The Pittsburgh Steelers, who won 35–28 on September 24, 1960.
6. Dallas tied the New York Giants 31–31 at Yankee Stadium on December 4, 1960.
7. 0–11–1
8. Kick returns, with 69.
9. After the winless 1960 season, Dallas scored 10 points in the final 56 seconds, including Allen Green's 27-yard field goal as time expired, to beat Pittsburgh in the 1961 season opener, 27–24. Ironically, Green had been cut by the Steelers a couple of weeks earlier. The paid attendance at the Cotton Bowl was 23,500.
10. True. Amos Marsh returned a kickoff 101 yards and Mike Gaechter returned an interception 100 yards, both for fourth-quarter touchdowns in a 41–19 win over visiting Philadelphia on October 14.
11. Tom Landry's 10-year contract extension was believed to be the longest in major pro sports history.
12. An overflow crowd of 76,251 at the Cotton Bowl watched Dallas lose to Cleveland 24–17 on November 21, 1965.
13. Dallas went 10–3–1 to win the 1966 Eastern Conference title, but lost the NFL Championship Game to Green Bay, 34–27.
14. Linebacker Chuck Howley is the only player from a losing team to be named MVP of the Super Bowl.
15. Ed "Too Tall" Jones. He was acquired in a trade from Houston for Tody Smith and Billy Parks.
16. Bob Lilly
17. On September 21, 1998, Deion Sanders returned a punt 59 yards for a touchdown and then a 71-yard interception for a touchdown against the New York Giants.
18. Running back Don Perkins on July 18, 1969.

Four

The Stadiums

When the Dallas Cowboys became an expansion franchise in 1960, they obviously didn't have their own stadium. However, the area did already boast the Cotton Bowl, which had been built in 1930. It originally seated 46,200 and cost $328,000.

By the time the Cowboys came around, upper decks on two sides had been added, bumping capacity to 75,504, and through the 1971 season the team compiled a 45–33–4 record there.

Built to replace the aging Cotton Bowl, Texas Stadium was constructed for $35 million. It opened on October 24, 1971, and had a seating capacity of 65,519. It also featured a unique partial roof that, in theory, protected fans from inclement weather while keeping the game outdoors.

It served as the franchise's home until work was completed on Cowboys Stadium in Arlington in 2009. The domed mega-facility with a retractable roof immediately gained numerous nicknames: Jerry's World, JerryWorld, Death Star, Six Flags Over Jerry, Boss Hog Bowl, and Cowboys Cathedral.

Quiz!

1. When the initial plans for Texas Stadium were drawn up in 1967, what was to be the minimum seating for when it opened in 1970?
    A. 54,000
    B. 58,000
    C. 62,000
    D. 70,000

2. Due to its unique hole-in-the-roof design, what was Texas Stadium nicknamed?

3. The first event at Texas Stadium featured what famous person?

4. How much did the Cowboys initially charge for suites at Texas Stadium? (Which was extensively criticized but over the long run turned out to be pretty cheap.)

5. Who scored the first touchdown in Texas Stadium, and which team did Dallas beat on October 24, 1971?

6. True or false? When Dallas defeated Denver in Super Bowl XII it was the first Super Bowl held indoors.

7. True or false? Dallas played in the most highly attended game in league history.

8. When was the last time the Cowboys didn't sell out a home game?

9. When was the last time Dallas didn't sell out on the road?

10. Which victory at Texas Stadium did Roger Staubach describe as "absolutely the most thrilling 60 minutes I ever spent on a football field"?

11. Who threw a 50-yard touchdown pass to Drew Pearson with 35 seconds remaining to beat Washington 24–23 at Texas Stadium in 1974?

12. Besides the snow and ice, for what was the 1993 Thanksgiving game against Miami best remembered?

13. Which reserve quarterback outdueled Brett Favre to pull off a 42–31 victory against Green Bay in 1994?

14. What was the Bounty Bowl and which team won at Texas Stadium?

15. Who carried the American flag above his head when Dallas took the field at Texas Stadium in the first game after the 9/11 terrorist attacks?
16. What off the field problem made the 1989 loss to Green Bay, 20–10, at Texas Stadium, memorable?
17. Who scored the final touchdown for the Cowboys at Texas Stadium?
18. What was the original estimated cost of Cowboys Stadium?
19. What did it end up being?
20. How many square feet are in the stadium?
21. In 2009, what was the inaugural event at Cowboys Stadium?
22. What was the first sporting event?
23. What was the first All-Star Game?
24. What was the first Super Bowl?
25. True or false? The Cowboys won their first regular-season game at Cowboys Stadium.
26. True or false? The Cowboys won their first playoff game at Cowboys Stadium.
27. How big was the initial video screen?
28. What problem was "discovered" during the first preseason game?
29. What was the smallest crowd the Cowboys ever played before? (Bonus: Name the non-NFL city where the game was played.)
    A. 10,000
    B. 12,682
    C. 4,954
    D. 12,370
30. When Dallas finally hosted its first Super Bowl (XLV) which two postseason rivals of the Cowboys played at Cowboys Stadium?

Answers:

1. B) 58,000. Owner Clint Murchison Jr. formally announced the plans on December 23, 1967.
2. The half-Astrodome.
3. Billy Graham
4. $50,000
5. Duane Thomas scored the first touchdown in Texas Stadium on a 56-yard run as part of a 44–21 victory over the New England Patriots.
6. True. The game was played at the Louisiana Superdome in New Orleans.
7. True. The 1994 American Bowl at Azteca Stadium in Mexico City, between the Cowboys and Oilers, attracted 112,376 fans.
8. The last non-sellout at home was December 16, 1990, against the Phoenix Cardinals.
9. The last road non-sellout was at the Arizona Cardinals, October 20, 2002.
10. The 35–34 win against Washington on December 16, 1979, when in his second-to-last game Roger Staubach threw two touchdown passes in the final four minutes, including an 8-yard pass to Tony Hill with 39 seconds remaining.
11. Backup quarterback Clint Longley.
12. After Jimmie Jones blocked a 47-yard field-goal attempt, Leon Lett tried to field the ball and instead kicked it toward the Cowboys' 1-yard line where Miami recovered and then kicked the game-winning field goal.
13. Jason Garrett.
14. Eagles coach Buddy Ryan allegedly offered $200,000 to anyone who knocked former Philadelphia kicker Luis Zendejas out of the game and $500 for Troy Aikman. The Eagles won 27–0 during Jimmy Johnson's first year.
15. George Teague.
16. The toilets froze in the stadium.
17. Jason Witten scored the final Cowboys touchdown at Texas Stadium on a 21-yard pass from Tony Romo.
18. $650 million.
19. Approximately $1.2 billion.
20. 3 million square feet, and it also covers 73 acres.
21. A country music concert headlined by George Strait that included Reba McEntire, Blake Shelton, and Lee Ann Womack.
22. A soccer Gold Cup quarterfinal game between Costa Rica and Guadeloupe.
23. On February 14, 2010, a record 108,000 attended the NBA All-Star Game.
24. Super Bowl XLV in 2011, the first the Dallas area hosted.
25. False, they lost 33–31 to the New York Giants.
26. True. On January 9, 2010, the 34–14 victory over Philadelphia ended a 13-year playoff drought.
27. The screen was 160 by 72 feet and stretches from the 20-yard line on both ends of the field.
28. Tennessee rookie A.J. Trapasso hit the video screen with a punt after repeatedly striking it during pregame warm-ups. The play was blown dead.
29. D) 4,954, vs. Minnesota, August 5, 1961, in Sioux Falls, South Dakota.
30. Green Bay Packers vs. Pittsburgh Steelers.

Five

Jersey Numbers

What's in a number? Sometimes a lot. When *Sports Illustrated* put together its list of the best NFL players by jersey numbers, five Dallas Cowboys were named, trailing only the Chicago Bears (nine), Pittsburgh Steelers (eight), and San Francisco 49ers (six), which had all been in the league longer.

The five selected were:

No. 8: Troy Aikman
No. 21: Deion Sanders
No. 22: Emmitt Smith
No. 48: Daryl Johnston
No. 54: Randy White

Numbers are important. Could anyone see Aikman playing in, say, No. 16? Didn't think so.

The incomparable 21, Deion Sanders, celebrates yet another interception.

The following questions are regarding jersey numbers through the 2009 season.

1. Who is the only player to have worn No. 74 in Cowboys history?
2. Which two numbers have been worn by just two players? (Bonus: Who wore them?)
3. Which number has been worn by the most players?
4. Who has worn Roger Staubach's No. 12 since he retired?
5. What two numbers did quarterback Wade Wilson wear?
6. Who is the only Dallas player to have worn four different numbers for the Cowboys? (Bonus: What were the numbers?)
7. What two other players wore three different numbers with the Cowboys? (Bonus: What were their numbers?)
8. What number did quarterback Craig Morton wear from 1965–74?
9. Which wide receiver wore the same number? (Hint: He also wore No. 19)
10. Who was the first player to wear No. 16 for the Cowboys?
11. Who was the most recent player to wear No. 16 for the Cowboys?
12. What number did Jason Garrett wear as a quarterback?
13. Who was the first player to wear No. 1 for the Cowboys?
14. Prior to the 1994 season no player had ever worn No. 69. Who was the first?
15. Who wore No. 00?

Answers:

1. Bob Lilly
2. 8, Buzz Sawyer and Troy Aikman; and 13, Jerry Rhome and Mike Vanderjagt.
3. 80: 21 players have worn it through 2010.
4. Nobody.
5. No. 18 and No. 11.
6. Tight end James Whalen wore No. 46, 81, 82, and 83 from 2000–03.
7. Wide receiver Cornell Burbage wore No. 15, 82, and 89, and cornerback Alundis Brice wore No. 21, 23, and 29.
8. No. 14.
9. Austin Miles.
10. Quarterback Steve Pelluer, 1984–88.
11. Quarterback Vinny Testaverde, 2004.
12. No. 17.
13. Kicker Efren Herrerra, 1973, 1976–77.
14. Tackle George Hegamin (1994–97).
15. No one.

Six

Nicknames

For those of you paying close attention, you're already aware that the original nickname proposed for the Dallas Cowboys was the Dallas Steers.

What's in a nickname? Well, steers are castrated male cattle.

Granted, it was used for a minor-league baseball team, as fans also once cheered for the Dallas Hams and the Dallas Submarines, but someone decided well before the team suited up that it might not be the image the franchise wanted to portray for a high-profile football team.

Plan B was naming the team the Dallas Rangers. However, even though Major League Baseball wouldn't arrive until 1972, when the Washington Senators moved and changed their nickname to honor the law enforcement agency, there was a minor-league team being started at roughly the same time. The Dallas Eagles and their rival Fort Worth Cats were combined with the Dallas-Fort Worth Rangers competing in the American Association.

So, to avoid confusion it was on to Plan C: Cowboys.

 **Quiz!**

Try to come up with the popular nicknames for the following:

1. Flozell Adams
2. Marion Barber III
3. Leonard Davis
4. Mike Ditka
5. Cliff Harris
6. Bob Hayes
7. Thomas Henderson
8. Michael Irvin
9. Raghib Ismail
10. Daryl Johnston
11. Adam Jones
12. Ed Jones

13. Leon Lett
14. Bob Lilly
15. Eugene Lockhart
16. Harvey Martin
17. Don Meredith
18. Nate Newton
19. Terrell Owens
20. Deion Sanders
21. Roger Staubach
22. Clint Longley
23. Randy White
24. Dallas' defense in the 1970s

Answers:

1. The Hotel
2. The Barbarian
3. Bigg (yes, with two gs)
4. Iron
5. Captain Crash
6. Bullet
7. Hollywood
8. Playmaker
9. Rocket
10. Moose
11. Pacman
12. Too Tall
13. Big Cat
14. Mr. Cowboy
15. Hitting Machine
16. Beautiful
17. Dandy
18. The Kitchen
19. T.O.
20. Prime Time (also went by Neon Deion)
21. Captain Comeback
22. The Mad Bomber
23. The Manster
24. The Doomsday D

Seven

Records

In the Dallas Cowboys' media guide, the section on individual records begins with a bit of a disclaimer that should always be taken into consideration when it comes to NFL season and career statistics.

In 1960, the NFL regular season lasted just 12 games. This was probably a good thing for the first Cowboys fans, who endured a 0–11–1 season and last-place finish in the Western Division, having been outscored 369–177.

With the addition of the expansion Minnesota Vikings in 1961, the regular season was increased to 14 games, which it maintained through 1977. In 1978, with some fans complaining about having to pay for several preseason games in addition to the regular season as part of their season-ticket packages, the league added two more games to the schedule in addition to a second wildcard team for the playoffs so that more teams would still be in contention for the postseason during the final weeks of the season.

Just something to keep in mind when looking over the numbers.

1. Who broke Don Hutson's league record for career receiving yards (7,991) with a 14-yard reception at Washington, giving him 8,000?
2. Who holds the Cowboys' record for passing yards in a single game?
3. Which tight end played in six consecutive Pro Bowls?
4. Who has the official and the unofficial team records for single-season sacks, which became an official league statistic in 1982?
5. Who did the team's official sack leader tie for the league record of sacks in consecutive games with 10?
6. In 1993, how many Cowboys were named to the Pro Bowl to set an NFC record?
7. Who played the most games in Cowboys history?
8. Who held the NFL record for career postseason rushing yards until Emmitt Smith reached 1,586 in 1999?
9. Who was the only player in NFL history to reach 1,000 rushing yards in 10 consecutive seasons until Emmitt Smith also did it?
10. Which NFL great did Emmitt Smith surpass to become the NFL's all-time leading rusher? (Bonus: How many yards did he have?)
11. Which three players were with the Cowboys for 15 seasons?
12. Who holds the Cowboys' record for career interception return yards? (Bonus: How many?)
13. Who holds the Dallas record for blocked kicks?
14. Who holds the record for blocked punts?
15. Who is the only player in NFL history to score more touchdowns than Emmitt Smith?
16. Who has the longest fumble return in Cowboys history?
17. Who has made the most solo tackles?
18. Who holds the Cowboys record among offensive players for Pro Bowl selections?

19. What's the team record for largest margin of victory?
20. True of false? Despite becoming the NFL's all-time leading rusher, Emmitt Smith didn't break the record for career carries.
21. True of false? The 1967 NFL Championship at Green Bay remains the coldest game played in league history.
22. Who holds the team record for passes intercepted in a single season?
23. What are the official, and unofficial, records for times sacked in a single season?
24. Who threw the longest touchdown pass in Cowboys history, who caught it, and for how many yards?

Name the individual team record holders in the following categories. (Bonus: List the numbers too.)
25. Career rushing yards
26. Career passing yards
27. Career passing touchdowns
28. Career receptions
29. Career receiving yards
30. Career interceptions
31. Career punting average
32. Career punt-return average
33. Career kick-return average
34. Career field goals
35. Career touchdowns

36. Career points
37. Season rushing yards
38. Season passing yards
39. Season passing touchdowns
40. Season receptions
41. Season receiving yards
42. Season interceptions
43. Season punting average
44. Season punt-return average
45. Season kick-return average
46. Season field goals
47. Season touchdowns
48. Season points
49. Game rushing yards
50. Game passing yards
51. Game passing touchdowns
52. Game receptions
53. Game receiving yards
54. Game interceptions
55. Game field goals
56. Game touchdowns
57. Game points
58. Outside of Emmitt Smith's career rushing record, which one of the previously-mentioned team records is also an NFL record?

Answers:

1. Billy Howton. He played most of his career with Green Bay and retired in 1963.
2. Don Meredith passed for 460 yards at San Francisco on November 10, 1963.
3. Jason Witten.
4. Because the NFL doesn't recognize sack totals before 1982, DeMarcus Ware's 20 in 2008 is the team record, but Harvey Martin had an unofficial 23 in 1977.
5. Denver's Simon Fletcher.
6. 11, of which seven started.
7. Ed "To Tall" Jones with 224, from 1974–78, and 1980–89.
8. Franco Harris with 1,556.
9. Barry Sanders.
10. Walter Payton (16,726 career rushing yards).
11. Ed "Too Tall" Jones (1974–78, 1980–89), Bill Bates (1983–97), and Mark Tuinei (1983–97).
12. Mel Renfro with 626.
13. Cornell Green blocked eight field goals from 1962–74.
14. Issiac Holt blocked four punts from 1989–92.
15. Smith had 175, 33 shy of Jerry Rice.
16. Greg Ellis had a 98-yard fumble return for a touchdown against Philadelphia on October 10, 1999.
17. Darren Woodson, with 787 tackles, 1992–2003
18. Larry Allen with 11.
19. 49 points: 56–7 vs. Philadelphia, October 9, 1966
20. False. He had 4,409 carries, easily topping Walter Payton's 3,838.
21. True. It was –13 degrees, with a –48 degree wind chill on December 31, 1967. The Packers won 21–17.
22. Eddie LeBaron and Danny White both had 25. LeBaron had that during the expansion team's first season in 1960, while White did so in 1980, his first year starting after Roger Staubach retired.
23. Drew Bledsoe was sacked 49 times in 2005. However Don Meredith was sacked 58 times in 1964 before it became an official statistic.
24. Don Meredith's 95-yard touchdown pass to Bob Hayes against the Washington Redskins in 1966 is still the longest touchdown pass in Cowboys history.
25. Career rushing yards: 17,162, Emmitt Smith
26. Career passing yards: 39,942, Troy Aikman
27. Career passing touchdowns: 165, Troy Aikman

28. Career receptions: 750, Michael Irvin
29. Career receiving yards: 11,904, Michael Irvin
30. Career interceptions: 52, Mel Renfro
31. Career punting average: 45.1, Mat McBriar
32. Career punt-return average: 13.3, Deion Sanders
33. Career kick-return average: 26.4, Mel Renfro
34. Career field goals: 162, Rafael Septien
35. Career touchdowns: 164, Emmitt Smith
36. Career points: 986, Emmitt Smith
37. Season rushing yards: 1,773, Emmitt Smith, 1995
38. Season passing yards: 4,483, Tony Romo, 2009
39. Season passing touchdowns: 36, Tony Romo, 2007
40. Season receptions: 111, Michael Irvin, 1995
41. Season receiving yards: 1,603, Michael Irvin, 1995
42. Season interceptions: 11, Everson Walls, 1981
43. Season punting average: 48.2 Mat McBriar, 2006
44. Season punt-return average: 20.8, Bob Hayes, 1968
45. Season kick-return average: 30.0, Mel Renfro, 1965
46. Season field goals: 34, Richie Cunningham, 1997
47. Season touchdowns: 25, Emmitt Smith, 1995
48. Season points: 150, Emmitt Smith, 1995
49. Game rushing yards: 237, Emmitt Smith, October 31, 1993
50. Game passing yards: 460, Don Meredith, November 10, 1963
51. Game passing touchdowns: Five, done many times
52. Game receptions: 15, Jason Witten, December 9, 2007
53. Game receiving yards: 250, Miles Austin, October 11, 2009
54. Game interceptions: Three, Herb Adderley, September 26, 1971; Lee Roy Jordan, November 4, 1973; Dennis Thurman, December 13, 1981; Terrence Newman, October 19, 2003.
55. Game field goals: Seven, Chris Boniol, Nov. 18, 1996; Billy Cundiff, Sept. 15, 2003
56. Game touchdowns: Four, done many times
57. Points: 24, done many times
58. The seven field goals in a game by Chris Boniol and Billy Cundiff.

Eight

Quotes

In 1979, the movie *North Dallas Forty* was released, a semi-fictional account of life as a professional football player loosely based on the Dallas Cowboys of the early 1970s.

Based on the novel written by Peter Gent, it stared Nick Nolte and Mac Davis. It also provided numerous memorable lines (many of which can't be repeated here) like, "Every time I call it a game, you call it a business. And every time I call it a business, you call it a game," and, "Ladies, ever had a quarterback sandwich?"

While some consider it the best football movie ever made, more than a few Cowboys fans have taken exception to the nonstop party atmosphere it portrayed. Still, no one can deny the brutally realistic tone of the film, such as in this famous exchange:

> Phil Elliott: Jo Bob is here to remind us that the biggest and the baddest get to make all the rules.
> Charlotte: Well I don't agree with that.
> Phil Elliott: Agreeing doesn't play into it.

No one ever accused the Cowboys of being dull.

Name who made the following statements:

1. "How 'bout them Cowboys!"

2. "When you want to win a game, you have to teach. When you lose a game, you have to learn."

3. "Coming to Dallas is like a breath of new life."

4. "If Tony Dorsett helps us win the Super Bowl, I don't care if they give him $2 million. If he doesn't help us win the Super Bowl, then he can give $1 million back."

5. "If it was third down, and you needed four yards, if you'd get the ball to Walt Garrison he'd get ya five. And if it was third down and ya needed 20 yards, if you'd get the ball to Walt Garrison, by God, he'd get you five."

6. "I know one thing, and I played with him, he changed the game. He made defenses and defensive coordinators work hard to figure out what you had to do to stop him."

7. "People don't understand what it took to be a fullback in our system—the sacrifices you made not just with your body, but your whole spirit. You took care of me as though you were taking care of your little brother. Without you, I know today would not have been possible."

8. "At that moment a voice came over me and said, 'Look up, get up, and don't ever give up. You tell everyone or anyone that has ever doubted, thought they did not measure up, or wanted to quit, you tell them to look up, get up and don't ever give up.'"

9. "A man like that comes along once in a lifetime. He is something a little bit more than great."

10. "His performances range anywhere from spectacular to spectacular. He could outmatch anybody's intensity from game to game."

11. "He's a perfectionist. If he was married to Raquel Welch, he'd expect her to cook."

12. "Consider yourselves sucked."

13. "He is one of the finest to ever play the game. I think if I had some of that Staubach competitiveness, I'd have been much better."

14. "Well, the man has balls. I'll say that. I don't know if they're brass or papier-mâché. We'll find out."

15. "I thought Jimmy Johnson's comment was insane. But I guess it was accurate."

16. "I was knocked senseless...The Cowboys seemed to be moving so much faster than we were...We were overmatched psychologically as well as physically."

17. "There were 11 men on the field and 10 of them knew what to do."

18. I had an intuition that if [Terrell] Owens scored again he'd do something crazy. I made up my mind that if he scores again and grandstands there'll be a fight. Before I knew it I whacked Owens pretty good. What I really appreciated was being quick enough to duck a 300-pounder who then went after me."

19. "Any one of 500 coaches could have won those Super Bowls."

20. "Gentlemen, nothing funny ever happens on the football field."

21. "That was the triumph of an uncluttered mind."

22. "Get your popcorn ready. It's going to be a show."

23. "Bless his heart. He's got to be the sickest man in America."

24. "If 'ifs' and 'buts' were candy and nuts, wouldn't it be a merry Christmas?"

25. "Leadership is getting someone to do what they don't want to do to achieve what they want to achieve."

26. "If the Super Bowl is the ultimate game, why are they playing it again next year?"

27. "Texas Stadium has a hole in its roof so God can watch his favorite team play."

28. "Turn out the lights. The party's over."

Answers:

1. Jimmy Johnson
2. Tom Landry
3. Mike Ditka
4. Roger Staubach, who made $250,000 annually, after Tony Dorsett signed a $1.1 million deal in 1977.
5. Don Meredith
6. Mike Ditka said it about Bob Hayes.
7. Emmitt Smith to former fullback Daryl Johnston during his enshrinement speech for the Pro Football Hall of Fame in 2010.
8. Michael Irvin during his 2007 enshrinement speech for the Pro Football Hall of Fame.
9. Tom Landry about Bob Lilly.
10. Tom Landry about Randy White.
11. Don Meredith about Tom Landry.
12. Bill Parcells
13. Bart Starr about Roger Staubach.
14. San Francisco coach George Seifert about Jimmy Johnson's guarantee of a victory.
15. Jerry Rice on Jimmy Johnson's guarantee of a victory.
16. Nick Buoniconti about Super Bowl VI.
17. Special teams coach Joe Avezzano said it about Leon Lett in the 1993 Thanksgiving game, a 16–14 loss to Miami.
18. George Teague
19. Without knowing the conversation was being recorded, Jerry Jones said it about Barry Switzer over drinks.
20. Tom Landry
21. Blaine Nye said it about Clint Longley's amazing Thanksgiving performance against the Washington Redskins.
22. Terrell Owens
23. Broadcaster Verne Lundquist said it about tight end Jackie Smith.
24. Don Meredith
25. Tom Landry
26. Duane Thomas
27. D.D. Lewis
28. Don Meredith, quoting a Willie Nelson song.

Nine

50 Years, 50 Questions

Anniversaries can be a tricky thing. Don't believe it? Try forgetting one and see what happens.

When the Dallas Cowboys celebrated their fifth year in the National Football League in 1964, they went 5–8–1 and had still not reached the playoffs.

The 10th year they went 11–2–1 and placed first in the Capitol Division of the Eastern Conference. However, for the third straight year Dallas couldn't get past the first game of the postseason, losing 38–14 to Cleveland in the conference championship (the Browns subsequently lost in the NFL championship to Minnesota, which lost to Kansas City in Super Bowl IV).

The franchise's "Silver Season" (25-year anniversary) wasn't exactly a memorable one either. The Cowboys went 9–7 to notch their 19th straight winning year, but missed the playoffs for the first time in 10 years and only the second time in 19 years.

Here's a question for each year of Dallas Cowboys history.

1960: Who led the Cowboys in passing their inaugural season?

1961: Which expansion team did Dallas face twice, in Weeks 2 and 4, and only give up one touchdown en route to a 3–1 start?

1962: What unusual scoring method did Pittsburgh benefit from in its 30–28 victory on September 23? (Note: The scoring difference is a strong hint.)

1963: True or false? After playing defensive tackle his first two seasons, Bob Lilly's career took off after being moved to defensive end.

1964: The trade of which kicker proved costly when rookie Dick Van Raaphorst struggled through the season?

1965: Which rookie sprinter used his speed to electrify fans while recording 1,003 receiving yards and 13 touchdowns?

1966: Which future NFL head coach signed a two-year deal as a free-agent halfback and ran for seven touchdowns, tied for second-most in the league, to help lead Dallas to its first postseason?

1967: True or false? With the addition of the expansion New Orleans Saints into the 16-team NFL, Dallas finished first in the four-team Capitol Division. (Bonus: Name the other divisions.)

1968: True or false? The NFL used to have a Runner-Up Bowl.

1969: Who led the 1969 Cowboys in rushing yards and attempts?

1970: Which two players had key interceptions to help lead Dallas past San Francisco in the NFC Championship Game?

1971: Although more associated with another team, which future Hall of Famer caught a seven-yard touchdown to put Super Bowl VI out of reach against the Miami Dolphins?

1972: Who was Dallas' first 1,000-yard running back?

1973: Which prominent Cowboy was named All-Pro for the first time in his 11th season?

1974: True or false? Dallas saw its string of playoff appearances snapped after eight years.

1975: Who caught Roger Staubach's 50-yard "Hail Mary" bomb to beat Minnesota in the first round of the playoffs, 17–14?

1976: Who set a club record for receptions by a tight end with 42?

1977: How many wins did Dallas start the season with to set a franchise record?

1978: Who scored the only non-offensive touchdown during Super Bowl XIII, a 35–31 victory for the Pittsburgh Steelers?

1979: What sport did Ed "Too Tall" Jones give up football for?

1980: Despite reaching the NFC Championship Game, what record did Tom Landry predict for his Cowboys that season?

1981: Who beat out Tony Dorsett for the league rushing title with 28 more yards than Dorsett's 1,646?

1982: What was Dallas' regular-season record during the strike-shortened season?

1983: Which player had a breakout season, with 46 receptions for 588 yards and six touchdowns? (Hint: Note the lack of the words "wide receiver" in the question)

1984: Who headed the 11-man group to purchase the Dallas Cowboys from Clint Murchison Jr.? (Bonus: What year did he sell the majority interest to Jerry Jones?)

1985: Which milestone did Tony Dorsett reach during a 27–13 victory against visiting Pittsburgh on October 13?

1986: Which team defeated the Cowboys 17–6 in the first American Bowl, at Wembley Stadium in London?

1987: Which prominent person in Cowboys history died on March 30 following a long illness?

1988: What rookie caught three touchdown passes in the final win of Tom Landry's career?

1989: Who became just the second head coach in the history of the Dallas Cowboys?

1990: True of false? Despite having a losing record, Jimmy Johnson was named the NFL Coach of the Year by the Associated Press.

1991: What were Emmitt Smith and Michael Irvin the first in NFL history to do?

1992: To what prominent league position was Jerry Jones appointed?

1993: By rushing for 1,486 yards, what did Emmitt Smith become just the fourth player in NFL history to accomplish?

1994: Who became just the third head coach in Dallas Cowboys history, and what previous connection did he have with the man he replaced?

1995: How many rushing touchdowns did Emmitt Smith score to break John Riggins' single-season NFL record?

1996: True of false? With nine Pro Bowl selections in 1996, Dallas set an NFL record with 41 players over a four-year period.

1997: What career milestone did Michael Irvin become just the 14th player in NFL history to reach?

1998: Against which rival did Emmitt Smith become the NFL's all-time rushing touchdown leader, breaking Marcus Allen's record of 123?

1999: How many rushing yards did Emmitt Smith tally at Minnesota while setting the NFL record for postseason rushing yards with 1,586? (Look closely for a hint.)

2000: Which Dallas player knocked San Francisco wide receiver Terrell Owens off the star when he tried to celebrate at midfield after scoring a touchdown?

2001: When Troy Aikman announced his retirement, how many team passing records did he hold or share?

2002: Which team was Dallas playing when Emmitt Smith became the NFL's all-time leading rusher?

2003: Which coaching legend was hired, which Cowboys legend was released, and which league legend died, all before the season started?

2004: Who announced his retirement after 12 seasons with the Cowboys and had the franchise record for career tackles?

2005: What all-time home attendance milestone did Dallas reach?

2006: Which Pro Bowl player was the holder who bobbled the ball on a field-goal attempt with 1:19 remaining, and on the subsequent scramble came up a yard short of a first down (two yards shy of the end zone), in a 21–20 loss to Seattle in an NFC wildcard game?

2007: Who was named the AP Comeback Player of the Year?

2008: Who scored the final touchdown at Cowboys Stadium, which was also the longest running play by an opponent at the stadium?

2009: Which 40-year-old quarterback threw four touchdown passes in a playoff game for the first time during his illustrious career, and in the process ended Dallas' season?

2010: Which free-agent rookie fullback had two brothers playing in the NFL?

Answers:

1960: Eddie LeBaron, who was acquired in a trade, completed 111 of 225 passes for 1,736 yards with 12 touchdowns and 25 interceptions.

1961: The Minnesota Vikings, 21–7 and 28–0.

1962: For the first time anyone could remember, points were awarded for a penalty when the Steelers were awarded a safety after Dallas was called for holding in the end zone on a 99-yard touchdown pass from Eddie LeBaron to Frank Clarke.

1963: True

1964: Sam Baker, who was sent to Philadelphia.

1965: Bob Hayes

1966: Dan Reeves

1967: True. The other three divisions were the Century, Western and Coastal.

1968: True. For example, in 1968 the Cowboys won the Capitol Division for the second straight year, but lost at Cleveland 31–20 on December 21 in the Eastern Conference Championship. Dallas won the Runner-Up Bowl over Minnesota, 17–13.

1969: Calvin Hill

1970: Lee Roy Jordan and Mel Renfro.

1971: Mike Ditka

1972: Calvin Hill became the first Dallas player to rush for 1,000 yards when he gained 111 on December 9 against the visiting Washington Redskins. He finished the regular season with 1,036 on a record 245 carries.

1973: Lee Roy Jordan

1974: True. The 8–6 Cowboys finished third in the NFC Eastern Division behind St. Louis and Washington, with the Redskins the lone wildcard team.

1975: Drew Pearson

1976: Billy Joe DuPree

1977: Eight

1978: Mike Hegman scored on a 37-yard return off a Terry Bradshaw fumble.

1979: Boxing

1980: 8–8. Instead they went 12–4.

1981: George Rogers of the New Orleans Saints, with 1,674 yards.

1982: 6–3

1983: Tight end Doug Cosbie.

1984: H.R. "Bum" Bright. He sold the majority interest to Jerry Jones in 1989.

1985: Dorsett became just the sixth player in NFL history to rush for 10,000 career yards.

1986: The Chicago Bears.

1987: Cowboys founder Clint Murchison. He was 63.

1988: Michael Irvin

1989: Jimmy Johnson

1990: True

1991: They were the first teammates to lead the NFL in rushing and receiving yards during the same season. Smith had 1,563 yards rushing, while Irvin set single-season club records for receptions (93) and receiving yardage (1,523).

1992: Jerry Jones was appointed to the NFL's Competition Committee by commissioner Paul Tagliabue, making him the first owner to do so since Cincinnati's Paul Brown.

1993: He became just the fourth man in NFL history to win three consecutive rushing titles.

1994: Barry Switzer. He was an assistant coach on the 1964 national championship team at Arkansas, where Jerry Jones and Jimmy Johnson were linemen.

1995: 25

1996: True. The next highest total was posted by the 1971–74 Miami Dolphins with 38.

1997: 10,000 receiving yards.

1998: The Washington Redskins.

1999: 99

2000: George Teague.

2001: 47

2002: The Seattle Seahawks.

2003: Bill Parcells was hired, Emmitt Smith released, and Tex Schramm died.

2004: Darren Woodson, who made 1,350 tackles.

2005: 20 million fans between the Cotton Bowl and Texas Stadium.

2006: Tony Romo

2007: Defensive end Greg Ellis.

2008: Le'Ron McClain of the Baltimore Ravens scored on an 82-yard run to cap a 33–24 victory.

2009: Brett Favre with the Minnesota Vikings.

2010: Chris Gronkowski. His brother Dan was a tight end with Denver and Rob played the same position with New England.

Ten

Draft/Trades

An interesting debate among Dallas Cowboys fans can always be had about which was the best draft in franchise history.

Most traditionalists consider it to be 1975, with defensive lineman Randy White was the second-overall selection followed by linebacker Thomas "Hollywood" Henderson 16 picks later; six other selections also won starting jobs for at least one season.

For what the 1964 draft lacked in numbers it more than made up with in big names. Second-round pick Mel Renfro, seventh-rounder Bob Hayes, 10th-rounder Roger Staubach all wound up in the Pro Football Hall of Fame, while guard Jake Kupp was named to the Pro Bowl.

Younger fans will point to 1989, when quarterback Troy Aikman was the first-overall selection and the Cowboys also landed fullback Daryl Johnston, center Mark Stepnoski, and defensive end Tony Tolbert.

However, a better and more challenging question is to name Dallas' worst draft. Here are some candidates:

1971: First-round pick Tody Smith, a defensive end, played two just two years for the Cowboys, while wide receiver Ron Jessie and defensive lineman Bill Gregory found success with other teams.

1978: Dallas' best pick was BYU fullback Todd Christensen. He was taken in the second round, but he broke his foot during the Cowboys' final exhibition game and was cut, only to go on to a stellar career as a tight end with the Oakland Raiders.

1982: Out of 16 picks, five made the team but only linebacker Jeff Rohrer and tackle Phil Pozderac becoming starters.

1995: Dallas traded out of the first round and primarily tried to add role players and backups.

2001: Numerous trades resulted in two second-round selections, quarterback Quincy Carter and safety Tony Dixon.

Tony Dorsett stabs his right foot into the ground and cuts left, leaving another Redskins defender empty-handed. *(Getty Images)*

**Quiz!**

1. Name the three players Dallas selected with the first-overall selection in the draft.
2. When Dallas became an expansion team in 1960, who was the Cowboys' first draft pick that year? (Note: We're going to be upfront on this one and tell you it's a trick question.)
3. What happened to Dallas' first draft pick in 1961?
4. So who was Dallas' first-ever choice?
5. Who was the first player Dallas selected with its own draft pick?
6. What did Dallas give up to acquire future Hall of Fame linebacker Chuck Howley from the Chicago Bears in 1961?
7. True or false? In 1963 the only player Dallas drafted in the first 10 rounds to make the team was Lee Roy Jordan.
8. Who was the only first-round draft pick not to play for the Cowboys?
9. What nickname was given to the 1975 rookies who made the Cowboys?
10. True or false? Dallas drafted Billy Cannon, the Heisman Trophy winner out of LSU.
11. Which team did Dallas trade with to acquire the 1977 first-round draft pick used to select Tony Dorsett?
12. What did Dallas get in return from the Denver Broncos for Tony Dorsett in 1988?
13. With which team did the Cowboys make "The Trade" on October 12, 1989?
14. What did Dallas give up?
15. What did the Cowboys acquire?
16. During the buildup to the trade, what alternate deal did Dallas consider, and which team ended up being outbid?
17. Despite already having Troy Aikman, which quarterback did Dallas take in the supplemental draft at the cost of the first pick in the 1990 draft?
18. Who did Dallas end up taking with the 17th selection in that same draft?
19. With which team did the Cowboys trade to acquire the No. 1 selection in the 1991 NFL Draft and select defensive tackle Russell Maryland?
20. After wheeling and dealing, how many picks did Dallas have for the 1991 NFL Draft, setting an NFL record for most selections in a 12-round draft?
21. In what round did the Cowboys draft quarterback Tony Romo?
22. How many draft picks did Dallas have in 2009?

Answers:

1. Defensive end Ed "Too Tall" Jones, 1974; quarterback Troy Aikman, 1989; and defensive tackle Russell Maryland, 1991.
2. No one. Dallas participated in an expansion draft, but not in the regular draft.
3. The Cowboys traded it along with a sixth-round selection to Washington for Eddie LeBaron.
4. Bob Lilly. Dallas sent Cleveland its first pick in 1962 for the Browns' selection at No. 13 overall.
5. Texas Tech linebacker E.J. Holub, with the 16th selection in the second round of the 1961 draft. He ended up signing with the team that drafted him in the AFL.
6. Dallas gave up a second-round and ninth-round draft choice in 1963 for Chuck Howley, who was making a comeback from what was believed to be a career-ending knee injury.
7. True
8. Texas defensive tackle Scott Appleton was the fourth-overall selection in 1964, the same draft in which Dallas selected three Hall of Famers, Mel Renfro, Bob Hayes, and Roger Staubach.
9. The Dirty Dozen.
10. False. But the Cowboys did take his son, a linebacker from Texas A&M with the same name in the first round of the 1984 draft (25th overall).
11. The expansion Seattle Seahawks.
12. A fifth-round pick.
13. The Minnesota Vikings.
14. Dallas traded away running back Herschel Walker and four draft picks: 1990 third-round pick (54th overall, Mike Jones); San Diego's 1990 fifth-round pick (116, Reggie Thornton); 1990 10th-round pick (249, Pat Newman); 1991 third-round pick, (68, Jake Reed).
15. Dallas received five players and eight draft picks. The players were linebacker Jesse Solomon, linebacker David Howard, cornerback Issiac Holt, running back Darrin Nelson (who was traded to San Diego after refusing to report), and defensive end Alex Stewart.
    As for the draft picks:
    Minnesota's first-round pick in 1990 (21) (traded this pick along with pick (81) for pick (17) from Pittsburgh to draft Emmitt Smith); Minnesota's second-round pick in 1990 (47) (Alexander Wright); Minnesota's sixth-round pick in 1990 (158) (traded to New Orleans); Minnesota's first-round pick in 1991 (conditional) (12) (Alvin Harper); Minnesota's second-round pick in 1991 (conditional) (38) (Dixon Edwards) Minnesota's second-round pick in 1992 (conditional) (37) (Darren Woodson); Minnesota's third-round pick in 1992 (conditional) (71) (traded to New England); Minnesota's first-round pick in 1993 (conditional) (13) (traded to Philadelphia).
16. Dallas nearly traded wide receiver Michael Irvin to the Oakland Raiders, but Minnesota ended up outbidding the Cleveland Browns for Herschel Walker.
17. Steve Walsh
18. Emmitt Smith
19. The New England Patriots.
20. 17
21. Tony Romo wasn't drafted; he signed as a free agent.
22. 12, the most since the draft was shortened to seven rounds in 1994 and the most overall picks since selecting 15 players in 1992's 12-round draft. However, after trading away its only first-day pick, all 12 selections were third round or later.

Eleven

The Postseason

Although the Dallas Cowboys have participated in some amazing and epic playoff games—from the rivalry with the San Francisco 49ers to one of the best Super Bowls ever played—there's been nearly as many letdowns.

After being named an expansion team in 1960, fans had to endure five losing seasons before the Cowboys managed to go 7-7 in 1965, and then a year later finally made the postseason. However, they were in for more growing pains as the Cowboys lost to the Green Bay Packers 34-27. The Packers then went on to beat Kansas City in the first Super Bowl.

Another year brought another step, a playoff win against Cleveland, although the Browns turned the tables and ended Dallas' season in both 1968 and 1969.

It wasn't until 1970 that the Cowboys reached the promised land, Super Bowl V, only to be rebuffed again, this time by Baltimore.

Finally, in 1971 it was as if the logjam finally broke, with Dallas earning league respectability and superiority with its first Lombardi Trophy (named after the legendary coach died suddenly from cancer in 1970). The franchise now boasts five.

"Our Super Bowl VI that we won was the biggest game because it took a lot of pressure off," Bob Lilly said. "It was enormously satisfying because we won the game and it was a nucleus of players who had grown up together, always losing the big ones. Started out with nothing and we were still together, and it was really, really neat."

1. True or false? Prior to the 2010 season Dallas had made the most Super Bowl appearances with eight.
2. Name each Super Bowl opponent. (Bonus: Include each score.)
3. True or false? The Cowboys are the only team in the NFL with more Super Bowl MVPs than Lombardi trophies.
4. True or false? Dallas has played in a postseason game that went into overtime.
5. What's the longest play in Cowboys playoff history?
6. Only four players in NFL history have won both a Heisman Trophy and been named Super Bowl MVP. Which Dallas Cowboy did it? (Bonus: Name the other three.)
7. True or false? Dallas was the only NFC franchise to win a Super Bowl during the 1970s.
8. True or false? Dallas recorded the only shutout in Super Bowl history.
9. True or false? Shortly before Super Bowl XXX it was discovered that some Internet proxy servers were blocking the game's official Web site.
10. How many different Cowboys have scored a touchdown in a Super Bowl?
11. Name them.
12. In how many different stadiums have the Cowboys won Super Bowls?
13. Name them.
14. True or false? All three of the Cowboys' Super Bowl wins in the 1990s were broadcasted on CBS.
15. True or false? In all five Dallas victories in the Super Bowl the losing team never scored a touchdown in the end zone marked "Cowboys."

Answers:

1. True. The Steelers caught the Cowboys by playing the Packers in Super Bowl XLV.
2. Super Bowl V: Baltimore, L 16–13; VI: Miami, W 24–3; X: Pittsburgh, L 21–7; XII: Denver, W 27–10; XIII: Pittsburgh, L 35–31; XXVII: Buffalo, W 52–17; XXVIII: Buffalo, W 30–13; XXX: Pittsburgh W 27–17.
3. True, because linebacker Chuck Howley was the lone player to win the award while playing for a losing team in Super Bowl V, and Harvey Martin and Randy White were the only co-MVPs ever named, in Super Bowl XII.
4. False
5. Felix Jones made a 73-yard touchdown run against Philadelphia on January 9, 2010.
6. Roger Staubach. The other three were Jim Plunkett, Marcus Allen, and Desmond Howard.
7. True. During the 1970s the only NFC victories were by the Cowboys in Super Bowls VI and XII.
8. False. There's never been a shutout in a Super Bowl. Dallas came the closest in Super Bowl VI when it yielded just three points, making the Cowboys the only team in Super Bowl history to not give up a touchdown.
9. True, and if you don't understand why ask your parents.
10. 18
11. Duane Thomas, Lance Alworth, Mike Ditka, Drew Pearson, Percy Howard, Tony Dorsett, Butch Johnson, Golden Richards, Tony Hill, Mike Hegman, Billy Joe DuPree, Jay Novacek, Jimmie Jones, Michael Irvin, Alvin Harper, Emmitt Smith, Ken Norton Jr., and James Washington.
12. Five
13. Tulane Stadium (VI), Louisiana Superdome (XII), Rose Bowl (XXVII), Georgia Dome (XXVIII), and Sun Devil Stadium (XXX).
14. False. Actually, they were all on NBC.
15. It's strange, but also true.

Super Bowl V: Baltimore 16, Dallas 13

1. By what unusual score did Dallas beat Detroit in the conference playoffs en route to Super Bowl V?
2. Who made the interception to set up the game-winning touchdown against San Francisco in the 1970 NFC title game to send Dallas to its first Super Bowl?
3. Where was Super Bowl V played?
4. What two Super Bowl firsts were established before the game even started?
5. What color jerseys did Dallas wear and why?
6. True or false? Super Bowl V is sometimes referred to as either the "Blunder Bowl" or the "Stupor Bowl" because of all the miscues.
7. How many combined turnovers did the teams have?
8. How many interceptions did Chuck Howley have?
9. How long was Johnny Unitas' controversial touchdown pass?
10. Why was it controversial?
11. Which player fumbled near the goal line?
12. Why was it controversial?
13. What was the halftime score?
14. Who was Baltimore's head coach?
15. Who replaced an injured Johnny Unitas late in the first half?
16. Which team was favored?
17. What did the halftime show feature?
18. Who made the game-winning 32-yard field goal for Baltimore with five seconds remaining?
19. How much did each Dallas player receive as part of the loser's share for Super Bowl V?
20. What famous thing did Bob Lilly do after the loss in Super Bowl V?

Answers:

1. 5–0 on a very muddy field.
2. Mel Renfro
3. The Orange Bowl, Miami.
4. The championship game was played for the first time on artificial turf and it was the first year that the Super Bowl was played in a merged National Football League.
5. Dallas wore blue because at the time league rules specified that the designated home team had to wear their colored jerseys.
6. True. Bubba Smith refuses to wear his Super Bowl V ring because of the sloppy play.
7. 11
8. Two
9. 75 yards.
10. There was some question as to whether Mel Renfro actually tipped the ball after it bounced off Eddie Hinton's hands and into the arms of tight end John Mackey. At the time, the rules stated that a pass could not be complete if it was touched by two offensive players in succession without a defender touching the ball in between. With limited instant replay during games, fans had to wait a week for confirmation when *ABC's Wide World of Sports* showed the rotation of the ball had been changed by Renfro's hand.
11. Duane Thomas
12. When the pile up was sorted out, Dallas center Dave Manders was holding the ball.
13. Dallas led 13–6.
14. Don McCafferty
15. Earl Morrall replaced an injured Johnny Unitas late in the first half.
16. Dallas was favored by 2½ points.
17. Florida A&M's band.
18. Jim O'Brien, who was a rookie.
19. $7,500. A year later, when Dallas defeated Miami, the winner's share was $15,000 per player.
20. Lilly ripped his helmet off and hurled it into the air.

Super Bowl VI: Dallas 24, Miami 3

1. True or false? Dallas' reputation during the 1971 season was that it couldn't win big games.
2. Which team was favored in Super Bowl VI?
3. True or false? The quarterback controversy was so deep that Roger Staubach and Craig Morton would frequently alternate plays.
4. True or false? Roger Staubach ended up leading the league in passing.
5. How did offensive lineman Ralph Neely get hurt in November, and who started in his place?
6. Heading into the Super Bowl, how many touchdowns had the Cowboys defense given up over the previous 25 quarters?
7. Who called head coach Don Shula at 1:30 A.M., after the Dolphins had just won the AFC Championship Game, and suggested a play for the Super Bowl?
8. What nickname did Tom Landry unintentionally give the Dolphins defense?
9. Who refused to talk to reporters during Super Bowl media day?
10. Who was the first player in NFL history to score touchdowns in back-to-back Super Bowls?
11. How many fumbles did Miami running backs Larry Csonka and Jim Kiick lose during the regular season?
12. How many Dolphins possessions did it take for Larry Csonka to lose a fumble? (Bonus: Who recovered it?)
13. True or false? Miami had more points in the third quarter than first downs.
14. True or false? Dallas' 252 rushing yards set a Super Bowl record.
15. Which Miami standout came into Super Bowl VI with a broken left hand and broke his right wrist during the game, but never came out?
16. When the Dolphins reached midfield in the fourth quarter, who made the interception and why didn't he score on the return?
17. Instead, who scored the final touchdown of Super Bowl VI?

18. Who was named the Super Bowl MVP?
19. Which quarterback passed for more yards in Super Bowl VI, Roger Staubach or Bob Griese?
20. Which American musical icon was saluted during the halftime show?
21. True or false? The game was blacked out in the host city of New Orleans.

Answers:

1. True
2. Dallas was favored by six points.
3. False, although they did alternate plays against the Chicago Bears with not-so-great results. Tom Landry settled on Roger Staubach and started him the final seven games of the season.
4. True. Roger Staubach had a 101.8 passer rating after throwing for 1,882 yards with 15 touchdowns and just four interceptions.
5. Ralph Neely broke his leg in a dirt bike accident and was replaced by Tony Liscio, ahead of future Hall of Famer Forrest Gregg, who was playing a final season with the Cowboys.
6. One. It was scored by the Minnesota Vikings during their 20–12 loss in the NFC Divisional Playoffs.
7. President Richard Nixon, who suggested a specific play to wide receiver Paul Warfield. Shula called it late in the first quarter only to have the pass broken up by Mel Renfro.
8. The "No-Name Defense," which came from Tom Landry being asked about Miami's defense and said that he couldn't recall any of the players names but they were a big concern.
9. Upset that the Cowboys would not renegotiate his contract after his rookie year, Duane Thomas had stopped talking to the press and to almost everyone on the team.
10. Duane Thomas
11. One, and it was by Jim Klick.
12. Larry Csonka committed his first fumble of the season on Miami's second possession and it was recovered by linebacker Chuck Howley.
13. False. The Dolphins failed to score any points or even get a first down.
14. True. The Cowboys set Super Bowl records for the most first downs (23), the least total yards allowed (185), and the fewest points allowed (three).
15. Safety Larry Scott. Of wearing casts on both hands for three months, said, "When I go to the bathroom, that's when I find out who my real friends are."
16. Chuck Howley made the interception, but tripped and fell at the Miami 9-yard line despite having nobody near him.
17. Mike Ditka, on a 7-yard reception.
18. Roger Staubach, who completed 12 of 19 passes for 119 yards and two touchdowns.
19. Bob Griese had 15 more yards on the same number of completions.
20. Louis Armstrong. The halftime show featured performances by Ella Fitzgerald, Carol Channing, Al Hirt, and the U.S. Marine Corps Drill Team.
21. True. It was the last time it was the last Super Bowl to be blacked out in the TV market in which the game was played.

Super Bowl X: Pittsburgh 21, Dallas 17

1. True or false? Super Bowl X was the first game played on AstroTurf at the Orange Bowl.
2. Which team was favored?
3. What was the nickname of Pittsburgh's defense?
4. Of Pittsburgh's 11 defensive starters, how many were named to the Pro Bowl? (Bonus: Name them.)
5. The emergence of which two players led to better passing numbers for Terry Bradshaw?
6. Who led the Cowboys in interceptions during the regular season?
7. Which quarterback, Terry Bradshaw or Roger Staubach, had more passing yards during the regular season? (Bonus: Who had more touchdown passes?)
8. Which quarterback had more passing yards in the game? (Bonus: Who had more touchdown passes and who had more passes intercepted?)
9. What injury in a conference championship game nearly had a major impact on Super Bowl X?
10. Who said of him, "I'm not going to hurt anyone intentionally. But getting hit again while he's running a pass route must be in the back of [his] mind. I know it would be in the back of my mind."
11. Who was named MVP of Super Bowl X?
12. True or false? Terry Bradshaw never saw the game-winning touchdown because after throwing the ball he was hit in the head and knocked out of the game.
13. Who was covering Lynn Swann on his acrobatic 53-yard reception?
14. What happened on the first snap of the game, and foreshadowed its outcome?
15. How many times was Roger Staubach sacked and who led the Steelers in that category?
16. After Steelers punter Bobby Walden fumbled the snap, who caught a touchdown pass on the very next play to open the scoring?

17. Who blocked the punt for a safety to spark the Steelers?
18. Who made the interception in the end zone as time expired?
19. What was the overall theme of the Super Bowl?
20. Which group performed during halftime? (Bonus: What was the name of the halftime show?)
21. Scenes for what movie were filmed during Super Bowl X?

Answers:

1. False. It was the last game played on AstroTurf at the Orange Bowl. It had been installed in 1970, but replaced with grass after Super Bowl X.
2. The Steelers were favored by seven points.
3. The Steel Curtain.
4. Eight: Defensive linemen Joe Greene and L.C. Greenwood; linebackers Jack Ham, Jack Lambert, and Andy Russell; and defensive backs Mel Blount, Glen Edwards, and Mike Wagner. Green was named to the Pro Bowl despite missing six games due to an injury.
5. Wide receivers Lynn Swann and John Stallworth. Both saw little playing time the previous season.
6. Linebacker Lee Roy Jordan led the team with six interceptions.
7. Roger Staubach had passed for 2,666 yards and 17 touchdowns, while Terry Bradshaw threw for 2,055 yards and 18 touchdowns.
8. Terry Bradshaw completed 9 of 19 pass attempts for 209 yards and two touchdowns with no interceptions, while Roger Staubach was 15-for-24 for 204 yards with two touchdowns and three interceptions.
9. Lynn Swann sustained a severe concussion in the AFC Championship Game against the Raiders and spent two days in a hospital.
10. Safety Cliff Harris.
11. Lynn Swann caught four passes for a record 161 yards, including the game-winning 64-yard touchdown pass in the fourth quarter.
12. True. Larry Cole made the hit and Terry Bradshaw didn't know what happened until after he had been helped to the locker room.
13. Cornerback Mark Washington.
14. L.C. Greenwood sacked Roger Staubach to force a fumble (that Dallas recovered).
15. Seven, with L.C. Greenwood notching three.
16. Drew Pearson
17. Steelers running back Reggie Harrison.
18. Pittsburgh safety Glen Edwards.
19. United States Bicentennial.
20. Up with People ("200 Years and Just a Baby: A Tribute to America's Bicentennial")
21. *Black Sunday.*

Super Bowl XII: Dallas 27, Denver 10

1. True or false? Denver had defeated Dallas in the regular season.
2. True or false? Super Bowl XII was the first to be played inside.
3. True or false? It was the first Super Bowl to be played in the afternoon.
4. Who tossed the coin?
5. Which team was favored?
6. What was the main storyline heading into the game?
7. When Craig Morton initially left the Cowboys in 1974, which team did he play for?
8. Who was the coach of the Denver Broncos?
9. What were the two defenses nicknamed?
10. Who was making his third Super Bowl appearances with his third different team? (Bonus: Name the teams.)
11. True or false? Dallas lost three fumbles in the first quarter.
12. Which number was greater in the first half: Denver's turnovers or first downs?
13. Which non-quarterback threw the touchdown pass that completed the scoring?
14. What was the theme of the halftime show?
15. True or false? At the time, Super Bowl XII was the most watched show in the history of television.
16. Which number was greater in Super Bowl XII, the number of passes completed by Denver starter Craig Morton, the number of passes completed by Denver reserve Norris Weese, or the number of interceptions by Dallas defenders?
17. How many passes did Denver complete?
18. True or false? Super Bowl XII set records for the most penalties and fumbles combined?

19. What prominent player retired after Super Bowl XII?
20. Which two Broncos went on to have lucrative television careers, one as a football analyst?
21. What two "firsts" occurred with the awarding of the MVP award?
22. What else did Randy White celebrate that day, January 15?
23. What two "firsts" did Tony Dorsett accomplish that day? (Hint: Neither had anything to do with winning the Heisman Trophy.)
24. True or false? It was the final Super Bowl following a 14-game regular season.

Randy White sacks Broncos quarterback Craig Morton in Super Bowl XII. *(Getty Images)*

Answers:

1. False. It was the first time that two teams that played during the regular season met in the Super Bowl, but Dallas won 14–6 on the final weekend of the regular season with the 12–1 Broncos resting most of their starters after having already clinched home-field advantage in the playoffs.
2. True
3. False. It was the first played in prime time.
4. Red Grange. It was the first time someone other than a referee made the coin toss.
5. Dallas was favored by six points.
6. Denver quarterback Craig Morton had spent nine years with the Cowboys and had competed with Roger Staubach for the starting job. Morton had guided Dallas to Super Bowl V, but Staubach won the job the following year and was the MVP of Super Bowl VI.
7. The New York Giants.
8. Red Miller was in his first year as head coach of the Broncos.
9. Denver's defense was the "Orange Crush" while Dallas had the "Doomsday Defense."
10. Preston Pearson had also played for Baltimore in Super Bowl III and Pittsburgh in Super Bowl IX.
11. False. Dallas did have three fumbles, by Butch Johnson on a double-reverse, Tony Hill, and Tony Dorsett, but recovered all of them.
12. Denver had seven turnovers in the first half compared to three first downs.
13. Robert Newhouse connected with Golden Richards on a halfback option pass for a 29-yard touchdown.
14. The halftime show was entitled "From Paris to Paris of America" and featured performers Tyler Apache Belles, Pete Fountain, and Al Hirt.
15. True. More than 102 million people tuned in.
16. They all had the same number: four.
17. Eight
18. True. The Cowboys and Broncos were called for 20 penalties for 154 yards and 10 fumbles (of which six were lost).
19. Mel Renfro
20. Defensive lineman Lyle Alzado and linebacker Tom Jackson.
21. Randy White and Harvey Martin were named co-MVPs, marking the first time the award was split between two players, as well as the first time it went to a defensive lineman.
22. It was his 25th birthday.
23. Tony Dorsett became the first player to win a national championship in college one year and the Super Bowl the next—and he did it in the same building. Pittsburgh won the 1976 national championship by defeating Georgia in the Sugar Bowl on January 1, 1977, at the Louisiana Superdome.
24. True

Super Bowl XIII: Pittsburgh 35, Dallas 31

1. True or false? Super Bowl XIII was the first rematch of a previous Super Bowl.
2. Which team was favored?
3. What future Super Bowl–winning coach was a starter?
4. True or false? Dallas became the first team to appear in five Super Bowls.
5. Besides the Lombardi Trophy, what distinction was at stake during Super Bowl XIII?
6. How many players from Super Bowl XIII wound up being enshrined in the Pro Football Hall of Fame? (Bonus: Name them.)
7. How many non-players from Super Bowl wound up being enshrined in the Pro Football Hall of Fame? (Bonus: Name them.)
8. After playing his entire career with what organization did the Cowboys lure tight end Jackie Smith out of retirement?
9. True or false? Because they were the home team, the Cowboys had to wear their blue jerseys in Super Bowl XIII.
10. Who said before the game that "Bradshaw couldn't spell *cat* if you spotted him the C and the A?"
11. True or false? Terry Bradshaw's 318 passing yards and four touchdowns were both Super Bowl records.
12. True or false? Terry Bradshaw was the first player since the AFL-NFL merger to be named both Super Bowl MVP and the Associated Press MVP during the same season.
13. True or false? Terry Bradshaw had the league's best passer rating in 1978.
14. True or false? The Cowboys were the first defending champion to lose in the Super Bowl.
15. True or false? The Cowboys are the only team in Super Bowl history to score 30 points or more in a Super Bowl and still lose.
16. Since Super Bowl XIII, how many times has the title game featured two quarterbacks with two Super Bowl victories apiece?

17. Who recovered the onside kick to set up Dallas' final touchdown?
18. Who had the heartbreaking drop in the end zone that, combined with the extra point, could have tied the game?
19. Which referee threw the controversial flag on Benny Barnes for pass interference?
20. What did NBC show before Super Bowl XIII?

Answers:

1. True, the teams played in Super Bowl X.
2. The Steelers were favored by 3½.
3. Tony Dungy
4. True
5. The victorious team would be the first three-time Super Bowl winner.
6. From Pittsburgh: Terry Bradshaw, Franco Harris, Lynn Swann, John Stallworth, Mike Webster, Joe Greene, Jack Lambert, Jack Ham, and Mel Blount. From Dallas: Roger Staubach, Tony Dorsett, Randy White, Rayfield Wright, and Jackie Smith.
7. Six. From Pittsburgh: coach Chuck Noll and owners Art Rooney Sr. and Dan Rooney; From Dallas: coach Tom Landry, general manager/president Tex Schramm, and defensive coordinator Ernie Stautner, who was a Hall of Fame defensive tackle for the Steelers.
8. The Cardinals.
9. False. After losing Super Bowl V in their blue jerseys, the Cowboys persuaded the NFL to change the rule so the "home team" could choose to wear their dark or white jerseys.
10. Linebacker Thomas "Hollywood" Henderson.
11. True
12. True
13. False. It was Roger Staubach.
14. True
15. True
16. Zero
17. Dennis Thurman
18. Jackie Smith
19. Fred Swearingen
20. NBC preceded the game with the network premiere of *Black Sunday*, the 1977 movie that depicted a terrorist attack and used footage shot during Super Bowl X between the same two teams.

Super Bowl XXVII: Dallas 52, Buffalo 17

1. Super Bowl XXVII was the last Super Bowl at which popular venue?
2. Where was it originally scheduled to be played and why did it move?
3. True or false? The Cowboys had the league's best record during the regular season.
4. What epic win did Buffalo pull off in the AFC playoffs?
5. Which team was favored?
6. What kind of offense did Buffalo run?
7. What standout special teams player for Buffalo blocked a punt to help the Bills take an early lead?
8. Which defensive tackle snared a fumble in the air and dove into the end zone for a touchdown? (Bonus: Name who had the sack to force the fumble.)
9. Who scored the fastest pair of touchdowns in Super Bowl history? (Bonus: How far apart?)
11. True or false? Dallas won Super Bowl XXVII despite having the youngest team in the league.
12. True or false? Dallas went from 1–15 to the Super Bowl the following year.
13. Which holdover player from the Tom Landry era claimed he would often go into the huddle and meet teammates for the first time?
14. True or false? Super Bowl XXVII marked the first time that the two visiting teams in the conference championships both won.
15. How many times did the Bills turn over the ball in Super Bowl XXVII? (Bonus: How many Dallas points did it lead to?)
16. True or false? The combined 11 turnovers set a Super Bowl record.
17. Who started for Dallas at wide receiver opposite Michael Irvin?
18. Who was the MVP of Super Bowl XXVII?
19. Who nearly scored on a 65-yard fumble return but had the ball stripped away just before reaching the goal line?

20. Who caught him?

21. Why did Dallas argue that Buffalo's final touchdown should not have counted?

22. Who performed at halftime?

23. True or false? Jimmy Johnson became the first head coach to win both a national championship at the collegiate level and a Super Bowl.

25. A week later, at the Pro Bowl, what did an exhausted Troy Aikman do to be fined by the NFL?

Answers:

1. The Rose Bowl.
2. Sun Devil Stadium in Tempe, Arizona, but voters had turned down an initiative to create a Martin Luther King Jr. holiday. (It passed in 1992, resulting in Super Bowl XXX being awarded to Tempe.)
3. False. Dallas had to travel to San Francisco for the NFC Championship Game, where it beat the 49ers 30–20.
4. Frank Reich led a monstrous comeback against Houston, with Buffalo overcoming a 32-point deficit in the third quarter to win 41–38 in the first round.
5. Dallas was favored by 6½ points.
6. No-huddle
7. Steve Tasker
8. Jimmie Jones (Charles Haley had the sack).
9. Michael Irvin had touchdown catches just 18 seconds apart.
11. True
12. False. It took three years to go from 1–15 to the Super Bowl—1989 to 1992.
13. Linebacker Ken Norton Jr.
14. True
15. Nine, five fumbles and four interceptions, which led to 35 points.
16. False. The 11 turnovers tied the Super Bowl record of 11, set in Super Bowl V between Dallas and Baltimore.
17. Alvin Harper
18. Troy Aikman was the game MVP. He completed 22 of 30 passes for 273 yards, four touchdowns, and no interceptions.
19. Leon Lett
20. Don Beebe
21. The Cowboys argued that Frank Reich's 40-yard touchdown pass to Don Beebe should have been nullified because they thought the quarterback crossed the line of scrimmage, making it an illegal forward pass.
22. Michael Jackson. It was the first time that ratings actually went up during halftime.
23. True
25. He left the game early, without permission, to catch a flight.

Super Bowl XXVIII: Dallas 30, Buffalo 13

1. Where was Super Bowl XXXVIII played?
2. Which team was favored?
3. Who performed the coin toss and why?
4. Prior to the game, how many times had the same two teams met in consecutive Super Bowls?
5. Prior to the game, how many times had there been a rematch in the Super Bowl?
6. Which team did Buffalo beat in the AFC Championship Game? (Bonus: Which two future Hall of Famers that were that team's offensive leaders?)
7. What controversial thing did Jimmy Johnson do before the NFC Championship Game?
8. What was bothering Emmitt Smith in that game?
9. True or false? He didn't finish the game and ended up being hospitalized.
10. True or false? Dallas' fifth Super Bowl victory and seventh appearance at the end of the 1993 season were both NFL records at the time.
11. True or false? Despite its big-name players, Buffalo's defense ranked 28th in the league (then last), giving up 5,810 total yards.
12. Who was the league MVP despite missing the first two games of the season due to a contract dispute?
13. Who was the MVP of Super Bowl XXVIII?
14. Who had the key fumble and later said it "cost us the game."
15. Who played a key part in three turnovers, and had a 46-yard fumble return for a touchdown?
16. Who made the longest field goal in Super Bowl history, 54 yards?
17. True or false? Dallas led at halftime.
18. How many unanswered points did Dallas score in the second half?

19. Which Buffalo player said "This one is the worst" about the Bills' fourth straight Super Bowl loss?
20. What was the theme of the halftime show? (Bonus: Who performed?)
21. What landmark amount did it cost for a 30-second ad during the Super Bowl?
22. Which team did Buffalo join as the only four-time loser in the Super Bowl?

Answers:

1. Georgia Dome, Atlanta.
2. Dallas by 10½ points.
3. Joe Namath, to mark the 25th anniversary of Super Bowl III.
4. Zero
5. Three. Dolphins and Redskins met in Super Bowls VII and XVII, the Steelers and Cowboys in Super Bowls X and XIII, and 49ers and Bengals in Super Bowls XVI and XXIII.
6. Buffalo defeated Kansas City, which was led by Joe Montana and Marcus Allen, 30–13. Thurman Thomas had 186 rushing yards and three touchdowns.
7. Jimmy Johnson called an area radio show and guaranteed a victory against the rival 49ers. He was correct; Dallas prevailed 38–21.
8. He had 88 rushing yards and 85 receiving yards and scored two touchdowns despite playing with a separated shoulder.
9. False. Troy Aikman was knocked out of the game with a concussion.
10. True
11. True
12. Emmitt Smith. He recorded 1,486 rushing yards and nine touchdowns while catching 57 passes for 414 yards and another touchdown.
13. Emmitt Smith. He had 132 rushing yards on 30 carries and scored two touchdowns.
14. Thurman Thomas
15. James Washington, who was the nickel back.
16. Steve Christie
17. False. The Bills had a 13–6 lead.
18. 24
19. Andre Reed
20. "Rockin' Country Sunday," featuring country music performers Clint Black, Tanya Tucker, Travis Tritt, and Wynonna and Naomi Judd.
21. $1 million.
22. The Minnesota Vikings.

Super Bowl XXX: Dallas 27, Pittsburgh 17

1. Which team did Dallas defeat in the NFC Championship Game?
2. Where was Super Bowl XXX played?
3. True or false? It was the last Super Bowl played in a collegiate setting.
4. Which team was favored?
5. Who coached the Cowboys?
6. True or false? He became the first coach to win both a collegiate national championship and Super Bowl.
7. How many touchdowns did Emmitt Smith score in the game?
8. Smith became just the fifth player to score a touchdown in three different Super Bowls. Name the first four.
9. True or false? Emmitt Smith had a 100-yard rushing performance.
10. Which team gained more yards?
11. How many Neil O'Donnell passes did Dallas intercept?
12. Why was that so unusual?
13. True or false? Super Bowl XXX was the only Super Bowl in which Dallas didn't have a turnover.
14. Which unlikely player was named Super Bowl MVP?
15. With which team did he go on to sign a big free-agency contract?
16. Who was the "other" Dallas cornerback?
17. True or false? Dallas became the first team to win three Super Bowls in four years.
18. Which player became the first to win five Super Bowls?
19. Where was the presentation of the Lombardi Trophy made?
20. Although he didn't know it at the time, which prominent Dallas player scored in his last game?
21. Who had his helmet stolen after the game?

22. What was the theme of the halftime show and who headlined? (Bonus: How did the performer leave the stage?)

23. At the time, what was the only television program watched by more people in the United States than Super Bowl XXX?

Answers:

1. The Green Bay Packers, who defeated the reigning Super Bowl champion San Francisco 49ers in an NFC Divisional Playoff.
2. Sun Devil Stadium, Tempe, Arizona.
3. True. The stadium is on the Arizona State campus.
4. Dallas was favored by 13½ points.
5. Barry Switzer
6. False. Jimmy Johnson was the first. Barry Switzer won three national championships at Oklahoma (1974, 1975, and 1985).
7. Two
8. Lynn Swann, Franco Harris, Thurman Thomas, and Jerry Rice.
9. False. He finished with 49 rushing yards.
10. The Steelers outgained the Cowboys 310–254, 201–61 in the second half. Pittsburgh also had a significant edge in first downs, 25–15.
11. Three
12. Neil O'Donnell entered Super Bowl XXX as the NFL's career leader in fewest interceptions per pass attempt.
13. True
14. Cornerback Larry Brown, who made two interceptions that led to 14 points.
15. The Oakland Raiders.
16. Deion Sanders
17. True
18. Charles Haley, who had won two with San Francisco (XXIII and XXIV) and two previously with Dallas (XXVII and XXVIII).
19. For the first time the Lombardi Trophy was awarded on the field and not in the locker room.
20. Tight end Jay Novacek. He missed the following season due to back injuries and then retired.
21. Emmitt Smith. It was returned to him several weeks later.
22. "Take Me Higher" was a celebration of the game's 30-year anniversary and featured Diana Ross. She left the stage in a helicopter.
23. The final episode of *M*A*S*H*.

Twelve

Hall of Fame

In 1961, the decision was made to build the Pro Football Hall of Fame in Canton, Ohio, the birthplace of the American Professional Football Association in 1920. The association would later be renamed the National Football League.

Canton was also where Jim Thorpe, the first big-name athlete to play the game, started his professional career with the Canton Bulldogs in 1915.

Being enshrined is considered the highest honor than can be bestowed in the sport, as evidenced by that inaugural class in 1963: Sammy Baugh, Bert Bell, Joe Carr, Earl "Dutch" Clark, Harold "Red" Grange, George Halas, Mel Hein, Wilbur "Pete" Henry, Robert "Cal" Hubbard, Don Hutson, Earl "Curly" Lambeau, Tim Mara, George Preston Marshall, John "Blood" McNally, Bronko Nagurski, Ernie Nevers, and Thorpe.

Since then, the building was expanded in 1971, 1978, and 1995, and renovated in 2003 and 2008. Today numerous people associated with the Dallas Cowboys are forever honored there.

Quiz!

1. Put the Cowboys' contingency in the Pro Football Hall of Fame in order by the date of their induction, from the first to the most recent:

Troy Aikman	Tom Landry	Emmitt Smith
Tony Dorsett	Bob Lilly	Roger Staubach
Bob Hayes	Mel Renfro	Randy White
Michael Irvin	Tex Schramm	Rayfield Wright

2. List the jersey numbers for each Hall of Fame player:

Troy Aikman	Bob Lilly	Randy White
Tony Dorsett	Mel Renfro	Rayfield Wright
Bob Hayes	Emmitt Smith	
Michael Irvin	Roger Staubach	

3. There are six other Hall of Famers who briefly played for the Cowboys (one to three years). Name them.

Bob Lilly sacks quarterback John Brodie in the NFC Championship Game in Texas Stadium on January 2, 1972. *(Getty Images)*

Troy Aikman

1. Where was Troy Aikman born? (Bonus: Name the date).
2. What's Aikman's middle name?
3. What two colleges did he play for?
4. At which was he named an All-American?
5. Aikman finished his collegiate career ranked very high in one prominent statistical category. What was it?
6. What Major League Baseball team attempted to sign Aikman to a contract out of high school?
7. True or false? Aikman was the first overall player selected in the 1989 draft.
8. True or false? Aikman was the winningest starting quarterback of any decade with 90 of 94 career wins during the 1990s.
9. True or false? Aikman was named All-Pro three times.
10. Aikman was the first Dallas rookie quarterback to start a season opener since which Hall of Famer?
11. True or false? During his rookie year Aikman led Dallas to a 7–9 record.
12. True or false? During just his third season, Aikman led the NFC in completion percentage at 65.3.
13. In a 1994 NFC Divisional Playoff against the Green Bay Packers, who did Aikman complete a 94-yard touchdown pass to, which at the time was the longest play from scrimmage in NFL postseason history?
14. Which team did Aikman face in his final game?
15. In what sport was Aikman a part owner with Roger Staubach? And what Major League Baseball team did he become a part owner of?

Answers:

1. Aikman was born November 21, 1966, in West Covina, California.
2. Kenneth
3. Oklahoma and UCLA.
4. UCLA
5. Aikman was the third-rated passer in NCAA history.
6. The New York Mets.
7. True
8. True
9. False. Surprisingly he was named All-Pro only once, 1993, but was second-team twice, in 1994 and 1995. Aikman was also named to six Pro Bowls.
10. Roger Staubach.
11. False. The Cowboys went 1–15.
12. True
13. Alvin Harper
14. The Washington Redskins in 2000. He was hit by LaVar Arrington and sustained the tenth concussion of his career.
15. NASCAR with Hall of Fame Racing, and the San Diego Padres.

Tony Dorsett

1. When and where was Tony Dorsett born?
2. Where did Dorsett attend high school?
3. What position did he play before running back?
4. True or false? Dorsett was the first college back to run for 1,000 or more yards for four seasons and the first to gain more than 1,500 yards three times.
5. How many yards did Dorsett have when set the career NCAA rushing record?
6. What was Dorsett the last running back to do until Alabama's Mark Ingram in 2009?
7. What team was set to draft Dorsett and how did the Cowboys acquire him?
8. True or false? Dorsett rushed for more than 1,000 yards his rookie season.
9. True or false? Despite losing to the Pittsburgh Steelers in Super Bowl XIII, Dorsett was named the game MVP.
10. How many times did Dorsett rush for more than 100 yards, and of those games how many times did Dallas win?
11. True or false? During his first nine seasons with the Cowboys, Dorsett never missed a game due to injury.
12. With which team did Dorsett finish his career?
13. True or false? Dorsett topped Jim Brown in both career rushing yards and combined net yards.
14. How many NFL rushing titles did Dorsett win?
15. On January 3, 1983, what impossible-to-break NFL record did Dorsett set against the host Minnesota Vikings on *Monday Night Football*?
16. True or false? The Cowboys had only 10 men on the field for the play.

17. True or false? The touchdown provided the game-winning points for the Cowboys.
18. How many rushing yards did Dorsett accumulate to set the Dallas single-season record in 1981?
19. What did he credit for his success that season?
20. What prompted Dorsett's retirement in 1989?

Answers:

1. April 7, 1954, in Rochester, Pennsylvania.
2. Hopewell High School near Aliquippa, Pennsylvania.
3. Linebacker
4. True
5. Dorsett had 6,082 career yards. His best season, as a senior, resulted in 1,948 rushing yards and 21 touchdowns.
6. Win both the Heisman trophy and the national championship the same season.
7. The second-year Seattle Seahawks were poised to select Dorsett with the second-overall selection in the NFL Draft, but instead traded it to Dallas for the Cowboys' first-round pick (No. 24 overall) and three second-round selections.
8. True. He had 1,007 rushing yards and 12 touchdowns and added 273 receiving yards and a touchdown on 29 catches to be named the NFL's Offensive Rookie of the Year.
9. False. However, he averaged six yards per carry for 96 rushing yards and his 140 total yards led all players.
10. Dorsett had 46 100-yard games, of which Dallas won 42 times.
11. False, but he was close, missing just three out of 142 games.
12. The Denver Broncos.
13. True. He finished with 12,739 rushing yards and 16,326 net yards.
14. Zero
15. Dorsett took a handoff up the middle and scored a 99-yard touchdown.
16. True. Running back Ron Springs was on the sideline.
17. False. The Vikings still won the game 31–27.
18. 1,646
19. Dorsett participated in a summer workout regiment for the first time and reported to training camp in the best shape of his career.
20. A knee injury.

Bob Hayes

1. How old was Bob Hayes when he died on September 18, 2002?
2. What college did he attend?
3. What non-football distinction did Hayes achieve before joining the Dallas Cowboys?
4. What was his famous nickname?
5. What position did he play there?
6. How did Dallas acquire Hayes?
7. Which other team drafted Hayes?
8. True or false? Hayes answered concerns about whether a track star could succeed in football by catching 46 passes for 1,003 yards and scored 12 touchdowns his rookie season.
9. True or false? Hayes set a team record with 71 career touchdowns.
10. How many of his touchdown receptions were 50 yards or longer?
11. What defense was said to have been developed in an effort to slow Hayes?
12. How many times was Hayes named first- or second-team All-NFL?
13. True or false? Hayes finished his career with the Cowboys.
14. Who resigned from the selection committee in protest of the controversial decision to leave Hayes out of the Pro Football Hall of Fame in 2004?

Answers:

1. 59
2. Florida A&M
3. He won a pair of gold medals at the 1964 Olympic Games in Tokyo, earning him the title of "World's Fastest Human."
4. Bullet Bob
5. Running back
6. Hayes was selected as a future pick by the Cowboys in the seventh round of the 1964 NFL Draft, No. 88 overall.
7. Hayes was also selected as a future choice in the 14th round of the 1964 AFL Draft, 105th overall, by the Denver Broncos.
8. True
9. True
10. 19. He also had an 86-yard touchdown catch in a 1967 playoff game against the Cleveland Browns.
11. The bump-and-run.
12. Four
13. False, Hayes played one season, 1975, with the San Francisco 49ers.
14. *Sports Illustrated* writer Paul Zimmerman.

Michael Irvin

1. What's Michael Irvin's middle name?
2. True or false? He's the 15th of 17 siblings.
3. For which team did Irvin play college football?
4. What number did Irvin wear in college?
5. True or false? Irvin set school records for most career receptions (143), receiving yards (2,423), and touchdown receptions (26).
6. Who later broke his school-record 2,423 receiving yards?
7. True or false? Dallas finished 4–28 during Irvin's first two seasons.
8. In what statistical category did Irvin lead the NFL in 1988?
9. In 1995, when Irvin caught 111 passes for 1,603 yards, how many 100-yard games did he have, to set an NFL record?
10. From 1991–98, in which season did Irvin *not* have 1,000 receiving yards?
11. Irvin's 47 100-yard receiving games were the third most in NFL history behind which two Hall of Fame players?
12. True or false? Irvin was named All-Pro five straight years.
13. True or false? Irvin finished his career in the Canadian Football League.
14. How many Super Bowls did Irvin lose?
15. Where did Irvin play his last game and why did the rival fans cheer?
16. When Irvin was inducted into the Pro Football Hall of Fame, who presented him?
17. During the ninth season of *Dancing with the Stars*, how did Irvin do?

Answers:

1. Jerome
2. True
3. Miami Hurricanes
4. He wore No. 47.
5. True
6. Santana Moss
6. True
8. Yards per catch, with 20.4.
9. 11
10. Irving didn't have 1,000 yards in 1996; he only played in 11 games and had 64 catches for 946 yards.
11. Jerry Rice (65) and Don Maynard (50).
12. False. Actually, he was named All-Pro only once, 1991.
13. False
14. Zero
15. Philadelphia fans cheered Irvin being carted off on a stretcher after he went headfirst into the turf at Veterans Stadium in 1999. He sustained a cervical spinal cord injury and was subsequently diagnosed with spinal stenosis. He later told a talk show he accepted Eagles fans cheering his injury because he'd been "killing them for years."
16. Jerry Jones
17. He was the ninth contestant eliminated.

Tom Landry

1. True or false? Tom Landry's birthday was September 11.
2. Which other famous coach had the same birthday?
3. True or false? Landry died on his birthday.
4. With what unit did Landry serve during World War II?
5. True or false? Landry played briefly for the New York Yankees.
6. True or false? As a defensive back, Landry had 32 career interceptions in just 80 games.
7. True or false? Landry was an All-Pro player.
8. When Landry became the defensive coordinator of the New York Giants, who was the well-known offensive coordinator?
9. What well-known formation was he credited as inventing, and whom did he build it around?
10. What defensive innovation did he come up with while leading the Cowboys?
11. What coaching position did he create? (Bonus: Name the person who had it.)
12. To counter the defense he devised, what was he the first coach to use regularly on offense and who originally devised it?
13. What physical attribute did Landry like in linemen, which became a staple for all NFL teams?
14. How much was Landry's first contract worth?
15. What business did Landry run on the side in Dallas when he agreed to run the expansion team?
16. True or false? Landry won only one game his first season as a head coach.
17. After leading the Cowboys to their first winning season in 1966, how long was it until they experienced another losing season?
18. During that stretch, how many division titles did the Cowboys claim?
19. How many times did Tom Landry coach in the Pro Bowl?
20. Name five Landry assistants who became NFL head coaches.

21. Which two coaches have more than Landry's 270 wins (including playoffs)?
22. True or false? Landry was also a Methodist Sunday school teacher.
23. On what show did Landry pretend to be a Catholic missionary priest in 1959? (Bonus: Who else was on that episode?)
24. In 1983, Landry appeared in a national television ad for which company?

Answers:

1. True. Landry was born September 11, 1924 in Mission, Texas.
2. Paul W. "Bear" Bryant
3. False. He died on February 12, 2000, at the age of 75.
4. Landry was assigned to the 493rd Bombardment Group at RAF Debach, England, as a B-17 Flying Fortress bomber co-pilot in the 860th Bombardment Squadron. From November 1944 to April 1945, he completed a combat tour of 30 missions and survived a crash landing in Belgium after his bomber ran out of fuel.
5. True. But not baseball's version of the Yankees. He was a defensive back, punter, and kick returner with the 1949 New York Yankees in the All-America Football Conference.
6. True. He also had a 40.9-yard punting average.
7. True. He was named All-Pro in 1954.
8. Vince Lombardi. Landry served the Giants as a player-coach in 1954 and 1955 before becoming a full-time defensive coach from 1956 to 1959.
9. The 4–3 defense with Sam Huff, who was therefore the first middle linebacker.
10. The Flex Defense, which altered its alignment to counter what the offense might do.
11. To get an edge in preparation, Landry had Ermal Allen analyze game films and chart the tendencies of the opposition. Now every NFL team has quality-control coaches.
12. "Pre-shifting" where the offense would shift from one formation to the other before the snap of the ball, originally devised by Amos Alonzo Stagg.
13. Long arms, which allow for increased leverage in the pass rush.
14. 5 years, $34,000 a season.
15. Insurance
16. False, he went 0–11–1.
17. 20 years, 1986.
18. 13. This included five NFC titles and victories in Super Bowls VI and XII. The Cowboys also played in Super Bowls V, X, and XIII.
19. Five
20. Acceptable answers include Mike Ditka, Dan Reeves, John Mackovic, Dick Nolan, Gene Stallings, and Raymond Berry.
21. George Halas and Don Shula. Landry went 250–162–6 and his record including playoff games was 270–178–6.
22. True
23. *To Tell the Truth.* (Bonus: The episode included balloonist commander Malcolm Roth).
24. American Express.

Bob Lilly

1. Where was Bob Lilly born? (Bonus: Name the date)
2. Where did Lilly play college football?
3. What jersey number did he wear in college?
4. True or false? Lilly is in the College Football Hall of Fame.
5. Who was an inspiration in Lilly's life?
6. How many games did Lilly miss during his 14-year career?
7. True or false? Lilly was an All-NFL selection every year from 1964 through 1969, then again in 1971 and 1972.
8. How many times was Lilly named to the Pro Bowl?
9. How many times was Lilly named All-Pro?
10. True or false? Lilly was named the NFL's defensive player of the year in 1964.
11. What was Lilly named for the first time in 1970?
12. True or false? Lilly returned nine turnovers for touchdowns.
13. True or false? Lilly won three Super Bowl titles.
14. What famous unit was Lilly the foundation of?
15. What was the signature play of Lilly's career?
16. What day was declared "Bob Lilly Day" in Dallas?
17. True or false? Lilly was the first player to spend his entire career with the Cowboys and be elected to the Pro Football Hall of Fame.
18. When *The Sporting News* ranked the 100 greatest football players in 1999, where was Lilly ranked?

Answers:

1. Bob Lilly was born July 26, 1939, in Olney, Texas.
2. Texas Christian University
3. 72
4. True. During his career the Horned Frogs surrendered an average of just eight points per game.
5. Lilly's father, Buster, who was crippled in a motorcycle-automobile accident when he was 17.
6. One
7. True
8. 11
9. Seven
10. False. He was named rookie of the year, though.
11. It's a bit of a trick question. For the first time he was named second-team All-NFL instead of first-team.
12. False. He had four, a 17-yard interception return and three fumble recoveries.
13. False. He won just one.
14. The Doomsday Defense.
15. His 29-yard sack of Bob Griese in the Super Bowl.
16. November 23, 1975.
17. True
18. No. 10. The only defensive players ahead of him were Dick Butkus and Lawrence Taylor.

Mel Renfro

1. Where was Mel Renfro born? (Bonus: Name the date)
2. What's Renfro's middle name?
3. For which college did Renfro light it up as a track star?
4. What position did he play in college?
5. What was his first position with the Cowboys?
6. How many interceptions did Renfro make as a rookie?
7. After four years in the NFL, what position did he switch to?
8. True or false? Renfro was named to the Pro Bowl in each of his first 10 seasons.
9. Was Renfro ever named the Pro Bowl MVP?
10. Which Pro Bowl did he miss due to injury?
11. How many interceptions did Renfro make when he led the NFL in 1969?
12. True or false? Renfro still holds the team records for career interceptions and kick-return yards.
13. How many touchdowns did he score during his career? (Bonus: Name how he scored them.)
14. Despite being such an accomplished runner, how many carries did Renfro have during his NFL career?
15. True or false? Renfro only played in one Super Bowl.
16. How many conference championships did he suit up for?

Answers:

1. Rentro was born in Houston, Texas, on December 30, 1941.
2. Lacy
3. Oregon
4. Running back
5. Safety
6. Seven
7. Cornerback, which is very unusual. Usually cornerbacks switch to safety as they start to slow down.
8. True
9. Yes. In 1971 he played cornerback and returned two punts for touchdowns to lead the NFC to a 27–6 victory.
10. 1973
11. 10
12. True. He made 52 interceptions and averaged 26.4 yards on kick returns.
13. Six, three on interceptions, one on a punt return, and two on kickoff returns.
14. Eight
15. False. He played in four Super Bowls.
16. Eight

Tex Schramm

1. What's Tex Schramm's given name?
2. Despite that, what state was he born in?
3. What's his middle name?
4. What did Schramm major in at the University of Texas?
5. What two jobs did he have pertaining to his major and what was his legacy in that career?
6. What was Schramm's first job in the NFL?
7. How old was Schramm when he was hired by the Cowboys?
8. During his 29 years running the Cowboys, how many winning seasons and playoff appearances did Dallas have?
9. How many head coaches did the Cowboys have under Schramm?
10. True or false? Schramm held the Cowboys' voting right at league meetings, which is usually performed by team owners.
11. Which of the following were implemented during Schramm's 25 years as chairman of the NFL's Competition Committee?
    a. Moved the official game time to the scoreboard clock.
    b. Moved the hash marks toward the center of the field to aid offenses.
    c. Implemented stricter pass defense rules to influence scoring.
    d. Moved goalposts from the goal line to the end line in part due to safety concerns.
    e. Approved sudden-death overtime for breaking ties.
    f. Put microphones on referees to announce calls.

g. Made the head-slap illegal.

h. Implemented the in-the-grasp rule to protect quarterbacks.

i. Instituted instant replay to aid officials.

j. Passed the rule allowing quarterbacks to spike the ball.

k. All of the above.

l. None of the above.

12. True or false? Schramm once hired future NFL commissioner Pete Rozelle.

13. What delayed Schramm's addition to the Ring of Honor?

14. With which famous Texan was Schramm inducted into the Pro Football Hall of Fame as part of the Class of 1991?

15. When did Schramm die?

Answers:

1. Texas. It was also his father's name and where his parents met.
2. California. He was born in San Gabriel on June 2, 1920.
3. Earnest
4. Journalism
5. Sportswriter for the *Austin American-Statesman* and CBS, where he came up with the idea of broadcasting the 1960 Olympic Games at Squaw Valley, California.
6. Publicity director for the Los Angeles Rams
7. 39
8. 20 winning seasons and 18 playoff appearances.
9. One, Tom Landry.
10. True
11. K, all of the above.
12. True. He hired him to be the Rams' public relations director in 1952.
13. Strained relations with Jerry Jones. He was inducted posthumously.
14. Earl Campbell
15. July 15, 2003. He was 83.

Emmitt Smith

1. Where did Emmitt Smith play high school football?
2. True or false? Smith was named the national high school player of the year.
3. What number did Smith wear while playing for the University of Florida?
4. How many school records did he break with the Gators?
5. True or false? After holding out as a rookie, Smith signed in time for the regular season and still rushed for 1,000 yards.
6. True or false? Despite leaving Florida after his junior year, Smith went back to school while with the Cowboys and earned his degree.
7. In how many consecutive seasons did Smith reach 1,000 rushing yards?
8. True or false? Smith was the first player in NFL history to post five straight seasons with more than 1,400 rushing yards.
9. When that streak was snapped in 2002, by how many yards was Smith short?
10. Name the only two other players with seven straight 10-touchdown seasons to start their career.
11. How many regular-season 100-yard rushing performances did Smith have?
12. Against which opponent did Smith have the most rushing yards?
13. Which is a bigger number for Smith, NFL rushing titles or Super Bowls won?
14. For what season was Smith named both the league MVP and the Super Bowl MVP?
15. True or false? Smith is the only Dallas player to ever be named the Associated Press' NFL most valuable player.
16. For which team did Smith play his final games before retiring?
17. After breaking Walter Payton's career rushing record, how many yards did Smith finish with?
18. Who is the only NFL running back to be named to more Pro Bowls than Smith's nine?

Answers:

1. Escambia High School in Pensacola, Florida.
2. True. He scored 109 touchdowns in high school.
3. 22.
4. In three years he set 58 school records while rushing for 3,928 yards, scoring 36 touchdowns, and earning SEC Player of the Year honors in 1989.
5. **False, but he was close.** Smith rushed for 937 yards and scored 11 touchdowns to be named Offensive Rookie of the Year.
6. True
7. 11
8. True
9. 25
10. Jim Brown and LaDainian Tomlinson.
11. 78, which set a league record.
12. Smith tortured the Philadelphia Eagles more than any other opponent, for 2,466 rushing yards.
13. Four rushing titles, three Super Bowl wins.
14. 1993
15. True
16. The Arizona Cardinals.
17. 18,355
18. Barry Sanders

October 27, 2002: On this 11-yard run Emmitt Smith eclipsed Walter Payton as the NFL's all-time leading rusher. *(Getty Images)*

Roger Staubach

1. Where did Roger Staubach attend school before the Naval Academy?
2. What was Staubach's nickname in college?
3. Name two other nicknames by which he was sometimes called.
4. Who did Staubach beat out for the 1963 Heisman Trophy?
5. True or false? After college, Staubach served four years active duty in the navy, including one year in Vietnam.
6. How old was Staubach when he was an NFL rookie?
7. True or false? Staubach immediately became the primary quarterback when he joined the Cowboys.
8. Who caught his first pro touchdown pass?
9. Who did he replace in a playoff game in 1972 after missing most of the season with a shoulder injury?
10. Staubach was only of only three quarterbacks to have a passer rating above 100.00 for an entire season during the 1970s. Who were the other two?
11. How many fourth-quarter comebacks did Staubach lead for the Cowboys? (Bonus: How many were in the final two minutes?)
12. What was the primary reason for Staubach's retirement in 1979?
13. True or false? When he retired, Staubach's 83.4 NFL passer rating was the best ever.
14. How many times did Staubach lead the NFL in passing? (Bonus: Name the years.)
15. Against which team did Staubach throw the most touchdown passes?
16. Name someone who was enshrined along with Staubach into the Pro Football Hall of Fame on August 3, 1985.
17. True or false? Staubach is the only player in the Pro Football Hall of Fame who spent his entire career with the Cowboys.

Answers:

1. New Mexico Military Institute. He led the Broncos to a 9–1 record in 1960.
2. Roger the Dodger, or the Artful Dodger.
3. Captain Comeback or Captain America.
4. Roger Staubach's 1,356-point margin over Billy Lothridge of Georgia Tech is the seventh largest in Heisman history
5. True. He attended training camps when on leave.
6. 27
7. False. He didn't become Dallas' regular quarterback until his third season, in 1971.
8. Lance Rentzel
9. Craig Morton. Staubach threw two touchdown passes in the final 90 seconds to beat San Francisco, 30–28.
10. Kenny Stabler and Bert Jones.
11. Staubach led 23 come-from-behind victories in the fourth quarter, 17 in the final two minutes.
12. Despite putting up his personal bests in pass completions, passing yards, and touchdown passing during his final year, Staubach feared the lingering effects of recurring concussions.
13. True
14. Four: 1971, 1973, 1978, and 1979.
15. The New York Giants.
16. Pete Rozelle, Joe Namath, O.J. Simpson, or Frank Gatski.
17. False. Bob Lilly is also enshrined.

Randy White

1. Randy White was born in the city of what future rival?
2. Where did White play college football?
3. What was his initial position?
4. Who moved him his sophomore year?
5. What major award did White win in college?
6. In what state's Sports Museum and Hall of Fame is White inducted?
7. Who was the only player selected before White in the 1975 draft? (Bonus: Name how many Pro Bowls he was selected to.)
8. At what position did Dallas try him at during his first two seasons?
9. How many games did White miss during his 14-year career?
10. True or false? White had the unusual distinction of being named All-Pro more times than to the Pro Bowl.
11. Which number is greater: the number of Super Bowls that White played in or the number of sacks he made in Super Bowls?
12. The number 94 is special to White because:
    a. It was his jersey number at Maryland, and has since been retired.
    b. It's the year he was voted into the College Football Hall of Fame.
    c. It's the year he was indicted into the Cowboys' Ring of Honor.
    d. It's the year he was inducted into the Pro Football Hall of Fame.
    e. All of the above.
    f. None of the above.
13. True or false? He studied Thai Boxing under Chai Sirisute, the founder of the Thai Boxing Association of the USA.
14. True or false? White made more than 1,000 career tackles.
15. True or false? White played for another coach with the Cowboys other than Tom Landry.

Answers:

1. Pittsburgh
2. Maryland
3. Fullback
4. New coach Jerry Claiborne
5. White won both the Outland Trophy and the Lombardi Award, so both answers are correct.
6. Delaware
7. California quarterback Steve Bartowski was the first-overall pick by the Atlanta Falcons. (He played in two Pro Bowls.)
8. Middle linebacker.
9. One
10. False. He was chosen for both nine times.
11. Sacks. He had four in three Super Bowls.
12. E) All of the above.
13. True
14. True, he had 1,104 (701 solo).
15. False. White retired in 1988, which was also Tom Landry's last season.

Rayfield Wright

1. What is Rayfield Wright's real first name?
2. What's his nickname?
3. Which future Dallas player had the same nickname?
4. True or false? Wright didn't make the football team at Fairmont High School in Griffin, Georgia, where he attended high school.
5. Where did Wright attend college?
6. What state is that in?
7. What sport was he playing?
8. Who got Wright to quit his summer job at a mill to play football?
9. True or false? Wright wasn't drafted.
10. What two positions did Wright try before moving to right tackle for good when Ralph Neely was injured?
11. Which NFL legend did he line up against during his first start at right tackle?
12. What threatened his 1975 season and sidelined Wright in 1977?
13. How many Pro Bowls did Wright play in?
14. True or false? Wright was named to the NFL's All-Decade Team of the 1970s.
15. True or false? During Wright's 13-year career, Dallas had a 70.3 percent winning percentage during the regular season.
16. How many Super Bowls did Wright play in?
17. In 1999, when the *Fort Worth Star Telegram* rated the most important people in Dallas Cowboys history, what number was Wright?
18. To what was Wright appointed due to his involvement with at-risk, inner-city youths.

Answers:

1. Larry
2. Big Cat
3. Leon Lett
4. True
5. Fort Valley State
6. Georgia. It plays in the Southern Intercollegiate Athletic Conference (SIAC).
7. Basketball
8. Coach Stan Lomax
9. False. He was a seventh-round selection in 1967.
10. Tight end and defensive end.
11. Deacon Jones
12. Knee surgery.
13. Six
14. True
15. False. It was even better—74.1 percent.
16. Five
17. No. 20
18. The Juvenile Supreme Court in Arizona.

Thirteen

Ring of Honor

On November 23, 1975, during halftime of a 27–17 victory over Philadelphia, the Dallas Cowboys unveiled Bob Lilly's name and jersey number underneath the Texas Stadium press box. That began the Ring of Honor to recognize former players, coaches, and club officials who made outstanding contributions to the organization.

As the first honoree, Lilly donned his jersey once more and was showered with both applause and gifts, including a car, gun, and hunting dog. The brainchild of Tex Schramm, who was selected posthumously a few months after he died in October 2003, the Ring Honor is considered the team's top accolade.

**Quiz!**

1. As of 2011, how many Cowboys were in the Ring of Honor, but not the Pro Football Hall of Fame?
2. Name them.
3. List their jersey numbers.
4. Which two were finalists for the Pro Football Hall of Fame, but as of 2011 had not been elected by the selection committee?
5. How does someone get chosen for the Ring of Honor?
6. Who was the most controversial selection for the Ring of Honor?
7. List the first five people inducted into the Ring of Honor, in order.
8. How many times have two or more people been inducted together?

Answers:

1. Five
2. Don Meredith, Don Perkins, Chuck Howley, Lee Roy Jordan, and Cliff Harris.
3. Don Meredith, 17; Don Perkins, 43; Chuck Howley, 54; Lee Roy Jordan, 55; and Cliff Harris, 43.
4. Lee Roy Jordan and Cliff Harris.
5. Everyone in the Ring of Honor was selected by the person running the organization at the time, either president-general manager Tex Schramm or owner Jerry Jones. Schramm placed an emphasis on the character of the inductees.
6. Michael Irvin, due to off-field issues.
7. Bob Lilly, November 23, 1975; Don Meredith and Don Perkins, November 7, 1976; Chuck Howley, October 30, 1977; and Mel Renfro, October 25, 1981.
8. Four: Don Meredith and Don Perkins, November 7, 1976; Tony Dorsett and Randy White, October 9, 1994; Cliff Harris and Rayfield Wright, October 10, 2004; Troy Aikman, Emmitt Smith, and Michael Irvin, September 19, 2005.

Don Meredith

1. Where was Don Meredith born?
2. What was his real first name?
3. What was his nickname?
4. At what college was Meredith an All-American quarterback?
5. Which legendary coach heavily recruited, but didn't land, Meredith?
6. True or false? His No. 17 was retired by his alma mater.
7. Which team drafted Meredith?
8. Who did Meredith back up for two years?
9. How many times was Meredith named to the Pro Bowl?
10. At what age did he retire?
11. True or false? Meredith led the Cowboys to the Super Bowl.
12. What year did *Monday Night Football* debut with Meredith in the booth?
13. Who else made up the broadcast team?
14. What song did Meredith sing in the broadcast booth when the game's outcome was no longer in doubt?
15. Who originally recorded the song?
16. For what beverage was Meredith the commercial spokesman?
17. Where is the Fire Station Museum—in which the Don Meredith Exhibit is housed—located?

(Left to right) Bob Hayes, Tom Landry, and Don Meredith try to stay warm as they gather around a heater at Cleveland Municipal Stadium on December 20, 1968.

Answers:

1. Mount Vernon, Texas
2. Joseph
3. "Dandy" Don
4. Southern Methodist University
5. Paul W. "Bear" Bryant
6. True
7. The Chicago Bears, in the third round (32nd overall) of the 1960 draft.
8. Eddie LeBaron
9. Three
10. 31, after nine seasons.
11. False
12. 1970
13. Howard Cosell and Keith Jackson. It was Cosell who dubbed Meredith "Dandy Don."
14. "The Party's Over."
15. Willie Nelson in 1967.
16. Lipton Ice Tea.
17. Mount Vernon, Texas.

Don Perkins

1. Where was Don Perkins born and raised?
2. Where did he attend college?
3. In 1958, in what statistical category did he lead the nation?
4. Which future Pro Football Hall of Famer was his college coach?
5. True or false? Perkins' No. 43 was the first number retired in school history.
6. True or false? Before the Dallas Cowboys were awarded a franchise Perkins signed a personal-services contract for $10,000 with a $1,500 bonus.
7. Which team selected Perkins in the 1960 draft?
8. What was that team eventually awarded to settle the dispute?
9. True or false? Perkins didn't play in 1960 due to a contract dispute.
10. What major award did Perkins win in 1961?
11. True or false? Despite finishing in the top 10 in league rushing for eight straight seasons, Perkins said he was a blocker first and a runner second.
12. What accomplishment was Perkins the first to achieve in Cowboys history and against which team did he do it?
13. How many times did he achieve that accomplishment during his career?
14. How many times was Perkins selected for the Pro Bowl?
15. What was Perkins known for not doing with the Cowboys?
16. After Perkins retired, who replaced him in the starting lineup?
17. In addition to his broadcasting career, what other job did he have until 1985?

Answers:

1. Waterloo, Iowa.
2. New Mexico
3. Kick returns
4. Marv Levy
5. True
6. True
7. The Baltimore Colts, with selection No. 106 in the ninth round.
8. The Colts were compensated with the Cowboys' ninth-round selection in the 1961 draft.
9. False. He missed the season due to a broken foot sustained during training camp.
10. NFL Rookie of the Year.
11. True
12. Perkins had the first 100-yard rushing performance in team history, with 108 yards on 17 carries against the expansion Minnesota Vikings.
13. 10
14. Six
15. Finishing Tom Landry's annual mile run during training camp.
16. Walt Garrison
17. Perkins was the director of the Work Incentive Program for New Mexico's Department of Human Services.

Chuck Howley

1. Where did Chuck Howley attend college?
2. Besides football, what other sports did he letter in?
3. In what did he win a Southern Conference championship?
4. Which team drafted Howley in 1958?
5. What caused that team to trade him in 1961?
6. What position switch with the Cowboys helped Howley?
7. How many games and how many seasons did Howley play after his knee injury?
8. With Howley on the team, how many times did the Cowboys finish in the top seven in scoring defense and yards allowed?
9. True or false? Howley had a reputation for playing well in big games.
10. How many career interceptions did Howley have and how many were returned for touchdowns?
11. True or false? He had more fumble recoveries.
12. True or false? He set a league record with a 99-yard fumble recovery.
13. How many times was Howley named All-Pro?
14. What kind of business did Howley run after retiring from football in 1973?

Answers:

1. West Virginia
2. Diving, gymnastics, track, and wrestling.
3. One-meter diving.
4. The Chicago Bears took him in the first round of the 1958 draft.
5. Chuck Howley sustained what appeared to be a career-ending knee injury during the 1959 training camp, and when he decided to attempt a comeback the Bears traded him to the Cowboys.
6. Howley went from strongside to weakside linebacker because Dave Edwards had more upper-body strength.
7. 165 games over 13 seasons.
8. 10
9. True. He was named MVP of Super Bowl V and could have won the honor again in Super Bowl VI.
10. 25 interceptions, with four returned for touchdowns.
11. False. He had 18 fumble recoveries, 17 with the Cowboys.
12. False. But he had a 97-yard recovery against Atlanta in 1966.
13. Five
14. Howley ran a successful uniform rental business in Dallas before getting involved in breeding quarterhorses.

Lee Roy Jordan

1. Where did Lee Roy Jordan attend college?
2. True or false? In college he played linebacker and center.
3. True or false? He led his college team to back-to-back national championships.
4. How many tackles did Jordan have in his final college game?
5. With what pick did Dallas select Jordan in the 1963 draft?
6. How many seasons did Jordan play with Dallas?
7. Jordan formed one of the greatest linebacking units with which two other players?
8. What franchise career record did Jordan set?
9. True or false? Jordan was considered a little small for his position.
10. What nickname did teammates give Jordan?
11. What specific item to help him prepare for games at home did Jordan have written into his contract?
12. On September 26, 1971, what team record did he set against Philadelphia?
13. In 1973, what amazing accomplishment did Jordan pull off during a five-minute stretch against the Cincinnati Bengals?
14. How many career interceptions did Jordan have?
15. How many times was Jordan named to the Pro Bowl?

Answers:

1. Alabama
2. True
3. False. The Crimson Tide won the 1961 title, but just missed in his senior year, going 10–1.
4. 31, during Alabama's 17–0 victory against Oklahoma in the Orange Bowl.
5. Sixth overall.
6. 14
7. Chuck Howley and Dave Edwards.
8. Solo tackles, with 743.
9. True, he was 6'1" and 215 pounds.
10. Killer
11. A film projector.
12. 21 tackles.
13. He made three interceptions in the first quarter, returning one for a 31-yard touchdown.
14. 32, tied for third-most all-time among linebackers.
15. Five

Cliff Harris

1. Where did Cliff Harris play college football?

2. Where is that located?

3. In what round of the 1970 draft was Harris selected?

4. As a rookie, who did Harris beat out for a starting job at free safety?

5. Why did Harris miss the second half of his rookie season?

6. What did teammates nickname Harris?

7. How many times was Harris named All-Pro?

8. How many times did Harris play in the Super Bowl?

9. How many consecutive times was Harris named to the Pro Bowl?

10. How many career interceptions did he have?

11. Why did Harris retire in 1979 at the age of 31?

12. True or false? Harris is in the College Football Hall of Fame.

13. True or false? After football he and Charlie Waters ended up working for an electricity marketing company and wrote a book together.

14. Harris' son Matt played for what Southeastern Conference football team?

Answers:

1. Ouachita Baptist University
2. Arkadelphia, Arkansas, about 65 miles southwest of Little Rock.
3. He wasn't. The Cowboys signed him as a free agent and invited him to training camp.
4. Third-round draft pick Charlie Waters.
5. Military obligation. He returned in time for Super Bowl VI.
6. Captain Crash.
7. Four
8. Five
9. Six
10. 29
11. To concentrate on his business ventures.
12. False. However, he is in the NAIA Hall of Fame.
13. True. The book was called *Tales from the Dallas Cowboys*.
14. Matt Harris was a starting safety for Arkansas.

Fourteen

The Dallas Cowboy Cheerleaders

It just wouldn't be a book on the Dallas Cowboys without including the famous cheerleaders, by far the NFL's most popular unit.

In 2010, *Forbes* listed the Dallas Cowboys as the No. 2 most valuable sports franchise, and the highest in the NFL, being valued at $1.65 billion. Of that, the Dallas Cowboys Cheerleaders reportedly brought in an extra $1 million per season.

However, in terms of marketing and exposure, their influence may be immeasurable.

In addition to working the sidelines during games, for which each reportedly makes just $50, there's the popular Country Music Television (CMT) reality show *Making the Team*, the annual swimsuit calendar, and scores of off-field performances and personal appearances. From camps for kids to trips overseas in support of American troops, the cheerleaders have become an international icon.

A Cowboys cheerleader smiles at the camera as they line up along the sideline during Super Bowl XII. *(Getty Images)*

1. True or false? The Dallas Cowboys have always had cheerleaders.
2. True or false? The Cowboys have always had dance line–style cheerleaders like they do now.
3. In the 1960s, what was the cheer unit called?
4. Before that, who did Tex Schramm hire to be on the sideline?
5. Who held the first auditions for the new cheerleading unit?
6. How many women tried out?
7. How many were selected?
8. Who managed the squad?
9. What fabric are the current uniforms made out of?
10. Who came up with the original design of the uniforms?
11. True or false? The uniform is trademarked and may not be copied.
12. True or false? Each uniform is custom-made.
13. Who has made the uniforms?
14. What moment is credited with the cheerleaders taking off in popularity?
15. On what two television specials did the '77 squad appear during the spring of 1978?
16. In what magazine did a number of former Cowboys cheerleaders appear later that year?
17. Who starred in the 1979 television movie, *The Dallas Cowboys Cheerleaders*?
18. True or false? She went on to appear in the same magazine.
19. True or false? It became the second-highest-rated made-for-television movie in history.
20. What's the age limit for cheerleaders?
21. True or false? Cheerleaders are not allowed to hold other jobs.

Answers:

1. True
2. False
3. CowBelles & Beaux were high school students from the Dallas/Ft. Worth area.
4. Models. It didn't work, though, because they weren't athletic.
5. Texie Waterman. She was a high-profile dancer who also had a studio in Dallas.
6. 60
7. Seven
8. Tex Schramm had his assistant Suzanne Mitchell do it.
9. Polyester. It's even machine washable.
10. Dee Brock and Paula Van Waggoner.
11. True
12. True, but that isn't unusual for cheerleading at most levels.
13. Leveta Crager, and since she retired in 1996, Greg Danison.
14. During Super Bowl X, a television cameraman panned toward the sidelines during a break. One of the cheerleaders alertly noticed and essentially winked to 75 million live viewers.
15. The *Rock-n-Roll Sports Classic* on NBC and *The Osmond Brothers Special* on ABC.
16. *Playboy*, under the name Texas Cowgirls.
17. Jane Seymour
18. True
19. True
20. There is none.
21. False. To even apply, candidates must be attending college or hold at least a part-time job, but according to the official website "being a full-time mother and homemaker counts."

Fifteen

Miscellaneous

From the stadiums to the Super Bowls to the Hall of
Famers, just about every aspect of the Dallas Cowboys
has been covered, right?

Not even close.

This section will test your knowledge of Cowboys oddities
and eccentricities. We'll look at the one-hit wonders, the great
moments, and the forgotten stories of Cowboys lore.

Which Texas school has had the most players on the Cowboys?
Who is the only quarterback in Dallas Cowboys history to have a
0.0 passer rating in a game? Did the original owners of the Dallas
Cowboys purchase the rights to "Hail to the Redskins" and threaten
not to let the Redskins use it?

From Wrestlemania to mascots to backup quarterback
nicknames; Herschel Walker, The Catch, strike-shortened seasons,
and the Dallas Desperadoes, this chapter revels in the absurd and
unbelievable.

1. For years, who was considered the Cowboys' unofficial mascot?
2. Who were the Dallas Desperadoes?
3. Where did running back Marion Barber III play college football, and with whom did he split backfield duties?
4. What was backup quarterback Diron Talbert's nickname and why?
5. Through 2009, which college had had the most players on the Dallas Cowboys?
6. Which Texas school has had the most players on the Cowboys (and which has had the second-most)?
8. Who was the first Cowboys coach to have a career losing record?
9. True or false? Miles Austin was the first undrafted player in Cowboys history to record a 1,000-yard receiving season when he had 1,320 in 2009.
11. Which Dallas quarterback has the best career passer rating in the postseason?
12. Has Dallas even done a worst-to-first, going from last place in its division to the top the following season?
13. How many times have the Cowboys failed to reach the playoffs the year after winning the Super Bowl?
14. True or false? Dallas was the first non-divisional winner to play in a Super Bowl.
15. What unusual achievement did Dallas pull off against Philadelphia in 2009?
16. Who led the NFL in rushing during the strike-shortened season of 1982? (Bonus: How many yards did he have?)
17. Which 1985 opponent snapped Dallas' non-shutout string at 218 games?
18. In 1985, who became the NFL's first three-time interception leader?
19. In what statistical category did Herschel Walker lead the Cowboys during his first NFL season?
21. True or false? After a 21–10 loss to Atlanta during the 1987 season, owner Bum Bright blasted head coach Tom Landry, saying he was "horrified" by the play-calling.

22. Who made more than 200 tackles during the horrible 1–15 season of 1989?
23. During the 1989 season, which player did Jimmy Johnson accuse the Philadelphia Eagles of placing a bounty on?
24. When Troy Aikman sustained a separated shoulder against Philadelphia in 1990, who replaced him?
25. When Troy Aikman sustained a sprained knee in 1991, who replaced him?
26. True or false? The first season Michael Irvin wasn't sidelined by an injury he led the league in receiving yards.
27. In 1991, when Dallas made its first playoff appearance since 1985, which team did it defeat? Which team later ended the Cowboys' season?
28. Which number was greater during the 1993 regular season, Troy Aikman interceptions or Michael Irvin touchdowns?
29. Who is the only quarterback in Dallas Cowboys history to have a 0.0 passer rating in a game?
30. Which Cowboy is shown on the famous *Sports Illustrated* cover of Dwight Clark making The Catch?
31. Who was the special referee for the Battle Royal that included pro football players during Wrestlemania 2 in 1986?
32. When Tony Romo broke the Dallas Cowboys' single-season touchdown record for quarterbacks in 2007, whose record did he break?
33. Who did Herschel Walker run over while scoring his first touchdown for the University of Georgia?
34. True or false? At one time the original owners of the Dallas Cowboys purchased the rights to "Hail to the Redskins" and threatened not to let the Redskins use it.
35. What other position did quarterback Danny White play for the Cowboys?
36. True or false? Halfback Preston Pearson and wide receiver Drew Pearson are related.
37. Who had more 300-yard passing games: Roger Staubach or Danny White?
38. Who did Roger Staubach throw his final NFL pass to?

Three-time Pro Bowl quarterback Tony Romo scrambles for a first down.

Answers:

1. Crazy Ray. His real name was Wilford Jones.
2. An Arena League team also owned by Jerry Jones.
3. Minnesota, and Laurence Maroney
4. "The Mad Bomber" for bouncing passes off the coaching tower during training camp. It wasn't because he hit Roger Staubach in the locker room during training camp and was subsequently traded.
5. The University of Tennessee with 23.
6. Texas A&M with 18, while Texas has had 11.
8. Dave Campo.
9. False. Drew Pearson had 1,087 yards in 1974 and 1,026 in 1979. However, Austin's 11 touchdown receptions were the most by an undrafted player.
11. Troy Aikman had an 88.3 passer rating in the postseason, which ranks in the top 10 in NFL history.
12. No
13. Zero
14. False. The Kansas City Chiefs won Super Bowl IV against Minnesota despite not having won its AFL division.
15. It defeated the same opponent, the Eagles, three times during the same season.
16. Tony Dorsett, with 745.
17. The Chicago Bears, 44–0.
18. Everson Walls
19. Receiving, both catches (76) and yards (837).
21. True
22. Middle linebacker Eugene Lockhart
23. Kicker Luis Zendejas. The former Eagle insisted he had proof in the form of a taped conversation with a Philadelphia assistant coach.
24. Babe Laufenberg
25. Steve Beuerlein
26. True, 1,523 in 1991.
27. Dallas won at Chicago 17–13 in the first round, but then lost at Detroit, 38–6.
28. Michael Irvin had seven touchdowns while Troy Aikman had only six passes intercepted in 1993.
29. Anthony Wright against the Tennessee Titans in 2000.
30. Cornerback Everson Walls
31. Ed "Too Tall" Jones
32. Danny White
33. Future Cowboys safety Bill Bates.
34. True
35. Punter
36. False. There's no relation.
37. Danny White had 14 300-yard passing performances while Staubach only had six.
38. Guard Herb Scott, who was an ineligible receiver.

Sixteen

The Two-Minute Drill

We'll ease you into this.

Do you know why the Dallas Cowboys' 13–7 loss at FedEx Field to the Redskins in the 2010 season opener was so unusual?

Primarily, it was because they lost.

The Cowboys have the NFL's best opening-day winning percentage (.694), ahead of the Denver Broncos (.653), New York Giants and Jacksonville Jaguars (.600), and Chicago Bears (.588).

Dallas won 17 consecutive season-opening games from 1965–81, which is far and away the longest opening day win-streak in the history of the league, ahead of Miami (11, 1992–2002), Detroit (10, 1930–39), Chicago (nine, 1984–92), and the Baltimore Colts (eight, 1955–62).

In 27 all-time season openers on the road, Dallas posted a 19–8 record. The franchise won its first 11 road season openers (1967–84), before losing three straight from 1987–89.

Dallas has opened at Washington (five times) more often than any other place, followed by Cleveland and Pittsburgh (three), and Chicago and the St. Louis Cardinals (two).

That's a taste of what you'll find in this section.

When it comes to Dallas Cowboys trivia, these are some of the hardest of the hard—ones even the most die-hard fans struggle with.

1. In what four states did the Cowboys hold their first four training camps (1960–63)? (Hint: Texas is not one of them.)
2. What was the name of the Dallas Cowboys' first home game? (Hint: It wasn't a regular season game.)
3. In its first NFL Draft in 1961, how many draft picks did Dallas have, how many were traded away, how many of its selection signed with the AFL, and how many players ended up making the active roster?
4. Name them and the rounds they were selected.
5. Name the players acquired from other teams.
6. The dispute over which player led to the creation of the Governor's Cup series, and after being sued by the Houston Oilers what did the Cowboys give up to sign him?
7. Who was among the numerous people to recommend Tex Schramm to Clint Murchison Jr.?
8. Who did the Cowboys trade to Philadelphia for tight end Mike Ditka?
9. Name the teams the Cowboys had to beat to advance to each Super Bowl. (Bonus: Name the scores.)
10. Who was the last Tom Landry-coached player to retire from the NFL?
11. How many games did it take Troy Aikman to reach 10,000 passing yards and notch 302 completions, the second most in team history?
12. How many different players did Troy Aikman throw a touchdown pass to? (Bonus: Name the top five and how many each caught.)
13. Of Bob Hayes' 71 touchdown receptions, 19 were for 50 yards or more. How many teams did he burn in scoring them (not including the 1967 playoff game against the Cleveland Browns)?
14. Although he didn't come up with the "America's Team" tag, what was one of the initial ways Tex Schramm took advantage of it?

15. Only four times in league history has a team won back-to-back offensive rookie of the year awards. Who were the Cowboys to do it and in what years? (Bonus: Name the Cowboy who was part of a back-to-back combo with another team.)

16. In 2009, when Miles Austin finished third in the league with 1,320 receiving yards, it was the sixth-best season all-time among undrafted wide receivers. Name the top five. (Hint: One player is listed twice.)

17. Troy Aikman's first career touchdown pass was during Week 2 of his rookie season—a 65-yard completion to Michael Irvin. How long did it take for him to throw another touchdown pass to Irvin?

18. How many fumble returns did Bob Lilly have during his career?

19. True or false? More than 25 Dallas Cowboys also played in the USFL.

20. Name them and what teams they played for.

21. When the team's official website, DallasCowboys.com, decided to compile a list of the Top 50 players in team history as part of the team's 50-year anniversary, who was No. 1?

22. Name the rest of the top five in order.

23. Name the rest of the top 10.

24. Name the other 40 players.

25. Name the 25 players listed under honorable mention.

Answers:

1. Oregon, Minnesota, Michigan, and California. Specifically, Pacific University, St. Olaf University, Northern Michigan College, and California Lutheran College, which were all located near the locations of the first preseason games.

Here's a listing of all preseason camps through 2010:

1960: Pacific University, Forest Grove, Oregon
1961: St. Olaf College, Northfield, Minnesota
1962: Northern Michigan College, Marquette, Michigan
1963–89: California Lutheran College, Thousand Oaks, California
1990–97: St. Edward's University, Austin, Texas
1998–02: Midwestern State University, Wichita Falls, Texas
2001: River Ridge Sports Complex, Oxnard, California
2002–03: The Alamodome, San Antonio, Texas.
2004–06: River Ridge Sports Complex
2007: The Alamodome
2008: River Ridge Sports Complex
2009: The Alamodome
2010: The Alamodome and River Ridge Sports Complex

Hall of Famer Mel Renfro sits on the sideline during a 1971 game. *(Getty Images)*

2. In their Dallas debut, the Cowboys' first home game was in the Salesmanship Club preseason game.
3. Dallas had 20 picks in its first draft, traded four picks away, had four sign with the AFL and had five make the roster.
4. Bob Lilly (1), Sonny Davis (4), Don Talbert (8), Glynn Gregory (9), and Lynn Hoyem (19).
5. Eddie LeBaron, Gene Babb, and Fred Cone. Dallas also traded away its first pick in the 1962 draft to take Bob Lilly in the first round.
6. After both Houston and Dallas drafted Oklahoma tackle Ralph Neely, the Oilers sued, but in a settlement the Cowboys kept him in exchange for their first and second picks, along with two fifth-round picks in the 1967 draft, and cash. Dallas also agreed to play five preseason games against the Oilers, three in Houston, thus creating the Governor's Cup Series.
7. George Halas of the Chicago Bears.
8. Wide receiver Dave McDaniels.
9. In the NFC Championships Dallas defeated: 1970, San Francisco, 17–0; 1971, San Francisco 24–3; 1975, Los Angeles, 37–7; 1977, Minnesota, 23–6; 1978, Los Angeles, 28–0; 1992, San Francisco, 30–20; 1993, San Francisco 28–21; 1995, Green Bay 38–27.
10. Michael Irvin.
11. 52.
12. 27. Michael Irvin caught the most with 49, followed by Jay Novacek (20), Alvin Harper (16), Daryl Johnston (13), and Emmit Smith (11).
13. Hayes burned 11 different teams. Here's the total list the Elias Sports Bureau put together for the Pro Football Hall of Fame:

Date	Opponent	Yds.
October 10, 1965	Philadelphia Eagles	82
December 19, 1965	New York Giants	65
September 18, 1966	New York Giants	74
November 13, 1966	Washington Redskins	52
November 13, 1966	Washington Redskins	95
October 22, 1967	Pittsburgh Steelers	55
October 29, 1967	Philadelphia Eagles	64
November 23, 1967	St. Louis Cardinals	59
December 24, 1967	Cleveland Browns	86
September 15, 1968	Detroit Lions	50
November 3, 1968	New Orleans Saints	54
December 8, 1968	Pittsburgh Steelers	53
October 19, 1969	Philadelphia Eagles	67
September 27, 1970	New York Giants	58
October 25, 1970	Kansas City Chiefs	89
November 8, 1970	New York Giants	80
December 20, 1970	Houston Oilers	59
September 19, 1970	Buffalo Bills	76
November 25, 1971	Los Angeles Rams	51
December 12, 1971	New York Giants	85

14. Schramm distributed 100,000 souvenir calendars stamped with the term "America's Team."
15. Running backs Calvin Hill and Duane Thomas were named the AP Offensive Rookie of the Year in 1969 and 1970. (Bonus: Mike Ditka with the Chicago Bears in 1961.)
16. Rod Smith, 2000, 1602; Alfred Jenkins, 1981, 1,358; Wes Walker, 2009, 1,348; Rod Smith, 2001, 1,354; Gary Clark, 1991, 1,340.
17. Week 7 of his second season.
18. Lilly returned 18 fumbles for 109 yards.
19. True.
20. Arizona Outlaws: Luis Zendejas.
    Arizona Wranglers: Doug Dennison, Aaron Mitchell.
    Birmingham Stallions: Bill Roe, Cliff Stoudt.
    Boston Breakers: Mitch Hoopes.
    Chicago Blitz: Bruce Thornton.
    Denver Gold: Dave Stalls, Bruce Thornton.
    Houston Gamblers: Vince Courville, Todd Fowler, Tony Fritsch.
    Los Angeles Express: David Howard, Derek Kennard, Aaron Mitchell.
    Memphis Showboats: Jim Miller, Bill Roe.
    Michigan Panthers: Larry Bethea, John Williams.
    New Jersey Generals: Herschel Walker, Roger Ruzek.
    Oakland Invaders: Gordon Banks, Steve Wright.
    Oklahoma Outlaws: Efren Herrera.
    Philadelphia Stars: Steve Folsom.
    Pittsburgh Maulers: Glenn Carano, Bruce Huther.
    Portland Breakers: Broderick Thompson.
    Tampa Bay Bandits: Harry Flaherty, Nate Newton.
    Washington Federals: Reggie Collier.
21. Roger Staubach
22. 2. Emmitt Smith
    3. Bob Lilly
    4. Troy Aikman
    5. Tony Dorsett
23. 6. Randy White (1975–88)
    7. Michael Irvin (1988–99)
    8. Mel Renfro (1964–77)
    9. Larry Allen (1994–2005)
    10. Bob Hayes (1965–74)
24. 11. Rayfield Wright (1967–79)
    12. Lee Roy Jordan (1963–76)
    13. Chuck Howley (1961–73)
    14. Cliff Harris (1970–79)
    15. Drew Pearson(1973–83)
    16. Darren Woodson (1992–2003)
    17. Don Meredith (1960–68)

18. Don Perkins (1961–68)
19. Harvey Martin (1973–83)
20. Deion Sanders (1995–99)
21. Cornell Green (1962–74)
22. Charles Haley (1992–96)
23. DeMarcus Ware (2005–present)
24. John Niland (1966–74)
25. Jason Witten (2003–present)
26. Ed "Too Tall" Jones (1974–78; 1980–89)
27. Everson Walls (1981–89)
28. Jay Novacek (1990–96)
29. Charlie Waters (1970–78; 1980–81)
30. Nate Newton (1986–98)
31. George Andrie (1962–72)
32. Danny White (1976–88)
33. Erik Williams (1991–2000)
34. Calvin Hill (1965–78)
35. Herschel Walker (1986–89; 1996–97)
36. Tony Hill (1977–86)
37. Daryl Johnston (1989–99)
38. Billy Joe DuPree (1973–83)
39. Jethro Pugh (1965–78)
40. La'Roi Glover (2002–05)
41. Mark Tuinei (1983–97)
42. Leon Lett (1991–2000)
43. Flozell Adams (1998–2009)
44. Pat Donovan (1975-83)
45. Ralph Neely (1965–77)
46. Terrell Owens (2006–08)
47. Walt Garrison (1966–74)
48. Bill Bates (1983–2007)
49. Tony Romo (2003–present)
50. Mark Stepnoski (1989–94; 1999–2001)

25. Jim Jeffcoat   Frank Clarke   Roy Williams
    Doug Cosbie   Thomas "Hollywood" Henderson   Bob Breunig
    Alvin Harper   Dennis Thurman   Robert Newhouse
    Russell Maryland   Duane Thomas   Jerry Tubbs
    Larry Cole   Herb Scott   Dave Manders
    Ken Norton   Preston Pearson   Dave Edwards
    Greg Ellis   Eugene Lockhart   Dexter Coakley
    D.D. Lewis   Mike Clark   Butch Johnson
    Chris Boniol

Jerry Jones and Jimmy Johnson celebrate with the Super Bowl XXVIII trophy.

About the Author

Christopher Walsh has been an award-winning sportswriter since 1990, and currently covers the University of Alabama football program for BamaOnline.com. He's twice been nominated for a Pulitzer Prize, won three Football Writers Association of America awards, and received the 2006 Herby Kirby Memorial Award, the Alabama Sports Writers Association's highest honor. Originally from Minnesota and a graduate of the University of New Hampshire, he currently resides in Tuscaloosa.

To make comments, suggestions or share an idea with the author, go to http://whosno1.blogspot.com/.

The author would like to thank Tom Bast for spearheading this project, and to everyone at Triumph Books who worked on it.